D1738023

Destination Thinking

A Business Planning Guide for Executives and Managers: The Systems Thinking Approach®

By
Stephen Haines
Founder and CEO
Haines Centre for Strategic Management
(Founded in 1990 · Offices in Over 20 Countries)

– with –

Valerie MacLeod
Centre Global Partner
Calgary, Alberta

Terry Dean Schmidt
Certified Business Associate
Seattle, Washington

Three Target Audiences

- *Progressive leaders at all levels around the globe, in all sectors – public, private, and not-for-profits.*

- *Senior management teams for an organization's:*

  - *Divisions*
  - *Regions*
  - *Units*
  - *SBUs (Strategic Business Units)*
  - *LOBs (Lines of Business)*
  - *MPAs (Government Major Program Areas)*

- *Senior management teams of an organization's Major Functional Areas (MFAs):*

  - *IT*
  - *Manufacturing*
  - *HR*
  - *Financial*
  - *Marketing/Sales*
  - *Operations*
  - *Engineering*
  - *Administration*
  - *Legal / Regulatory*
  - *PR / Communications*
  - *Planning*

How to reach the authors:

Haines Centre for Strategic Management

1420 Monitor Road San Diego, CA 92110-1545 • Email: info@HainesCentre.com

Telephone: (619) 275-6528 • Fax: (619) 275-0324

Website: www.HainesCentre.com

Stephen Haines:

(619) 275-6528 • Stephen@HainesCentre.com

Valerie MacLeod

(403) 236-3928 • VMacleod@telusplanet.net

Terry Schmidt

(206) 433-0700 • Terry@managementpro.com

Dedication

This book is dedicated to the many executives, managers, and senior professionals we have had the privilege of working with since 1990, in improving this Three-Year Business Planning Framework. Clients have been our loyal "skeptics" and have become our best friends at the Centre. They have shown us, in many creative and unique ways, how to make this "System of Managing Strategically" a reality in their units, divisions, functions, and organizations.

Seventy-five percent of all major change fails, as noted in our 2005 book, *Enterprise-Wide Change*. Therefore, this book is dedicated to those in the top 25% of strategic leadership today.

In today's global economy, they are the future. Thank you for all you have taught me.

And thank you to my co-authors, Valerie and Terry, for your assistance with this book and your constant feedback to sharing this Strategic Thinking Framework in practical applications.

Stephen Haines
San Diego, California

ABOUT THE AUTHORS

Stephen Haines

"CEO, Entrepreneur, and Strategist"...
"Facilitator, Systems Thinker, and Author"

Stephen Haines is the founder and CEO of Haines Centre for Strategic Management® in San Diego, California. He is internationally recognized as a world-class leader in the field of Strategic Management and Change. Steve has over 30 consecutive years of CEO level experience with over 200 CEOs in complex and diverse international situations. The Centre's purpose is to assist CEOs in developing and sustaining high performance organizations in today's dynamic environment. The Centre has 38 Certified Master Consultants and Partners, with offices across the USA and Canada; and in 20 different countries around the globe.

Steve personally serves senior management and boards in a wide variety of private and public sectors. His career focus uses extensive "best practices" research to lead dozens of major consulting projects. These projects have included mergers and acquisitions, high growth, turn-arounds, restructurings, and strategic transformations. Steve specializes in strategic planning and transformational change. These changes include a strong emphasis on enhancing Leadership Competencies through executive coaching, leadership development, HR management, and executive team building. These organization-wide changes also include organization redesign to ensure the (1) realignment of delivery processes and (2) attunement of peoples' hearts and minds needed to create customer value.

From Steve's extensive research and 20+ years experience in Systems Thinking, the Centre has copyrighted state-of-the-art frameworks and processes for (1) "The ABC's of Strategic Management™" (Planning and Change), and (2) The Rollercoaster of Change™ concept and an "Organizational Systems Model" to guide strategic change. He is also the architect of a copyrighted Systems Thinking Approach™ to Centering Your Leadership℠ through "Leadership Development" and its six natural core leadership competencies found nowhere else.

Prior to founding the Centre, Steve was president and co-owner of University Associates Consulting and Training Services (a pioneer firm in the development of human resource practitioners and their organizations). He was the architect of its renewal before devoting full-time work in strategic management and change through Haines Centre.

In addition, Steve was executive vice-president for ICA, a diversified $14 billion nationwide financial services firm. Prior to that, he was senior vice-president of Freddie Mac, a $32 billion financial institution. Steve has been a member of eight top management teams – both US and International – with corporate responsibilities for all aspects of organizational functions, including planning, operations, marketing, PR, communications, finance, HR, training and facilities. His career included executive positions at MCI, Exxon, Sunoco, and Marriott Corporations.

Steve has an Ed.D. (ABD) in management from Temple University and an M.S.A. in organization development (minor in financial management) from George Washington University. He has a B.S. in engineering from the prestigious class of 1968 at the U.S. Naval Academy in Annapolis, MD (minor in foreign affairs), and is a graduate of the DOD Human Goals Institute. As a former Naval Officer, he has flown Navy jets, piloted ships, and served in Vietnam.

Steve is today's new breed of "world-class executive consultant" providing invaluable value-added advice as (1) a Master strategist and business expert; (2) a Systems Thinker; and (3) a leader with enormous skills in "facilitation" of difficult executive groups. He is an accomplished keynoter, as well as a prolific author, with over 15 books to his credit (and still growing).

Summary of the World Leader in Strategic Management
(The Systems Thinking Approach)

Steve's diverse background includes exposure to hundreds of firms and extensive "Best Practices" research. He has received numerous Who's Who honors, written 15 books, over 50 articles, and developed 11 volumes of the Centre's Tool Kits and Guides (7000 pages). He has taught over 80 different kinds of seminars and is in demand as an insightful keynote speaker at international conferences, with a special emphasis on CEO and Board issues. He is a premier TEC Organization resource (groups of 15 CEOs) with over 80 seminars to his credit. He was also the co-leader of the prestigious Banff Centre for Management's two week senior-most executive and leadership development course. He has also been on nine boards including chairman of a credit union and the national board of directors for the Association for Strategic Planning. His interests include family, community service, sports, sailing, travel, photography, art, design, and his grandson Sebastian.

Valerie MacLeod

Centre Global Partner, Planning Co-Practice Leader
Facilitator, Coach, Entrepreneur, Author, Strategist, Educator, Speaker
Calgary, Alberta, Canada

Valerie MacLeod runs the Centre's Calgary, Alberta, office as our Partner and Planning Co-Practice Leader. She is passionate about helping clients "plan their work and work their plan." Valerie is a skilled and insightful facilitator and coach with extensive expertise in the area of organizational effectiveness. Her dynamic coaching impacts business results by uncovering purpose, sharpening focus on "the big picture," and then providing clients with the tools they need to achieve success on their own. Valerie specializes in group facilitation and team dynamics. The tools she marshals for her clients include: strategic planning and implementation, change management, team-building, motivation, strategy alignment, performance management, and visioning. She works with boards, CEOs, executives, managers, and teams to clarify and achieve vision, values, and strategies. Valerie has an M.B.A. in Human Resources Organizational Development from the University of Calgary and a Bachelor of Mathematics degree from the University of Waterloo.

Terry Dean Schmidt

Centre Certified Business Associate -
Strategic Project Master, Author, and Change Agent
Seattle, Washington

Terry Schmidt is a Certified Business Associate of the Centre who manages our Seattle office. He brings 25 years of global experience as a business strategist and management consultant. Terry has assisted hundreds of organizations in 28 countries to become more strategic, productive, and profitable. His clients include Fortune 500 companies, fast-growing companies, national research organizations, and government agencies. Terry has an M.B.A. from Harvard and a B.S. in Engineering from the University of Washington.

Terry is a featured guest instructor at UCLA's esteemed Technical Management Program, where he teaches strategic planning. He is also a faculty member of the Los Alamos National Laboratory, where he teaches Strategic Project Management and helps technical teams plan complex projects that support national interests.

Table of Contents

"Insanity and Change"

Insanity...
is doing the same things,
the same way,
and expecting different results.

- Attributed to Albert Einstein

Change...
Effective change
takes two to five years,
even with concentrated and continual actions.

- Stephen Haines

Introduction and Forward

This book is for progressive leaders at all levels of organizations around the globe, and in all sectors – private, public, and not-for-profit. It is designed as a practical tool for you to develop and complete Three-Year Business Plans for your area of responsibility. It is aimed at three groups of progressive leaders.

1. While "Strategic Planning" is the key for all organizations at a corporate level, very often, the Division, Region, Units, SBUs, LOBs, etc., are not required to develop their own Strategic Plans. These Strategic Plans are called Three-Year Business Plans in the organizational hierarchy of planning, and they are crucial to your competitive success.

2. Furthermore, this book is designed to help leaders of government agencies and their Major Program Areas (MPAs) with their own Three-Year Business Plan. Government is much like big business these days, and it needs to function like a business in today's competitive environment (but without the need to generate profits).

3. Lastly, this practical book is designed to assist progressive leaders of staff support functions who also need Three-Year Business Plans. Heads of IT, Finance, Marketing & Sales, HR, and the like, should not be given a free ride strategically. Once they develop their own Three-Year Business Plans in support of the Organization, then they can become strategic thinkers, strategic planners, and strategic change leaders with a respected seat at the Chief Executive's head table.

Chapter 1 discusses the ABCs of Strategic Management™ based on The Systems Thinking Approach™ and science of General Systems Theory.

Chapter 2 covers our underlying assumptions (Three Main Premises) and the benefits our clients have achieved using our Systems Thinking Approach˚.

Chapter 3 briefly shows our copyrighted "Strategic Management System" in a logical (yet comprehensive) way. This will give you a clear overview picture of our approach using our Three Goals mentioned and Three Main Premises to be discussed as well.

Chapter 4 will discuss the crucial future environmental Scanning needs of today's dynamic global marketplace (Phase E). Chapter 5 will discuss in detail the first eight steps of Three-Year Business Planning within its A-B-C Phases.

Chapter 6 will finish the discussion of the last two steps of the "D" Phase of strategic change, thus completing the entire Strategic Management Process.

Chapter 7 will show you "how to get started" and Engineer Success Up Front in your own journey to creating a customer-focused high performance organization.

Keep in mind that we will discuss this Strategic Management System within the sequence of the Three Primary Goals:

- first strategic and Business Unit planning

- then successful strategic change management

- and lastly, sustaining high performance, year after year.

CHAPTER 1
Thinking Backwards to the Future: Destination Thinking

These days, everyone understands that rapid and tumultuous change is about the only predictable factor of the future. Death, taxes, and change are now the three constants in life. Perhaps at no other time have new ideas and prospects seemed so dazzling, nor the possible pitfalls so numerous and deep.

In the Industrial Age, public and private enterprises built their future by incremental expansion of present technologies, assumptions, and day-to-day operations. In today's global economy, the strategy of merely building on the same present is defunct.

This "More of the Same" (MOS) Syndrome is causing organizations, Lines of Businesses (LOBs), Strategic Business Units (SBUs), and Major Government Program Areas (MPAs) to shrink or die. It is also causing Major Functional Areas (MFAs) to become obsolete and irrelevant.*

Worldwide markets and instant global communications are multiplying the opportunities available to every enterprise, as well as consumers and employees. Today, organizations must keep pace with changes in their environment and overhaul current businesses, programs, and operations.

Organizations must be willing to completely reinvent their future vision and then begin thinking backwards to this future, fleshing out the strategies and actions needed to remain successful. They must also react to the changing values and demands of internal and external customers and employees, and they cannot forget the attunement of people's hearts – recognizing and supporting the intangible goals of personal growth, contribution, and fulfillment.

The danger of this dynamic "new reality" is that business units, functions, and governmental bureaucracies can be swallowed up before they know what is happening to them. In a troubled and rapidly changing economy, the mortality rate for the tradition-bound goes higher and higher while at the same time, high technology start-ups are creating whole new industries and millionaires.

*Author's Note: The term "Organization" will be used to refer to all of the different units throughout this book. Pick the one that you are interested in and read this from that perspective.

Within this "sea change" around the world, a new way to do Strategic Planning and Three-Year Business Planning has emerged. A new way to do Planning for government agencies and Major Functional Areas/departments. It springs from the science of Systems Thinking, based on 50 years of rigorous scientific work by General Systems Theorists (now known as The International Society for the Systems Sciences - www.ISSS.org). This change is coupled with a lifetime search by the author that led to the reinvention and creation of a new way to think, plan, and execute, in order to create your ideal future, despite the chaos and complexity of today's world. The key is "thinking backwards to the future" that creates an ABC-like "elegant simplicity" that can be used similarly by first time supervisors all the way up to senior executives and CEOs. It is quite simple, yet also a comprehensive and profound way to captures today's complexity and reduce it to its essence in a way that works.

In this guide, our focus will be on showing you how to accomplish the three primary goals of any business unit, government program, or functional support organization.

Three Primary Goals of Any Organization/Unit

GOAL #1:

Develop a Business Plan/Document

GOAL #2:

Ensure its Successful Implementation and Change

GOAL #3:

Build and Sustain High Performance
Over the Long Term, Year After Year

In order to show you how we assist organizations and units of all types, both public and private, in achieving these three goals, we have organized this book into our five A-B-C-D-E phases of Systems - The Natural Way the World Works.

The Organization/Unit as a System: A-B-C-D-E
(from Systems Thinking)

Every organization is a living system – a complex network of inputs, interactions, processes and outputs in today's dynamic, global environment. Therefore, management and organizations need a set of concepts and tools for wiring, fitting and aligning these concepts together with a sense of integrity of effort. Any organization/unit will function best when all these interactions, processes, departments and employees work together in an integrated, collaborative and cross-functional fashion, supporting the firm's overall Vision, Goals, Outputs, Results and Purposes (you pick the term; it does not matter). The organization/unit's Vision must be used to think, plan, act and communicate throughout the organization/unit to get Superior Results.

As indicated on the accompanying model and chart, our Organization as a Living System Model has five distinct phases: A,B,C,D,E. We call these phases the ABCs of Strategic Thinking™. The reason for this is that any system (and especially an unit or organization) can be described by five main phases (see following chart). This is because systems are made up of a set of components that work together for the overall objectives of the whole (outputs).

Thus:

A system is defined as a series of inputs to a throughput (or action processes), to achieve outputs within a given environment, along with a feedback loop to measure success (which is fed back as new Inputs).

Destination Thinking

Our A-B-C-D-E Phases use this definition and start with the Future, because we want to be proactive in creating our Ideal Future. Destination Thinking can be used, not only in Business Planning, but in a remarkably effective way in our daily lives. By thinking backwards, from your Ideal Future Destination to your present state, you can fundamentally change your life. Once you grasp this process, you can manage your life in a more proactive manner, just as excellent units and organizations do.

This is the "Core Technology" of the Science of Systems Thinking, and embodies the framework of this book. The first step to Systems Thinking Excellence and Destination Thinking is achieved by mastering the five Strategic Thinking questions illustrated on the next page.

THE SYSTEMS THINKING APPROACH®
"The Natural Way the World Works"

"A New Orientation to Life" – Our Core Technology
STRATEGIC THINKING
"From Complexity to Simplicity"

Systems: Systems are made up of a set of components that work together for the overall objective of the whole (output).

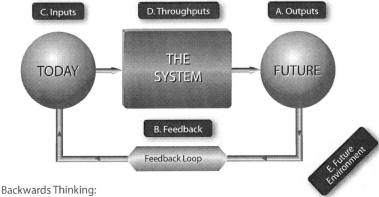

Backwards Thinking:
Five Strategic Thinking Questions – In Sequence:

A   Where do we want to be? (i.e., our ends, outcomes, purposes, goals, holistic vision)

B   How will we know when we get there? (i.e., the customers' needs and wants connected into a quantifiable feedback system)

C   Where are we now? (i.e., today's issues and problems)

D   How do we get there? (i.e., close the gap from C ➞ A in a complete, holistic way)

E   Ongoing:
What will/may change in your environment in the future?

vs. Analytic Thinking Which:

- Starts with today and the current state, issues, and problems
- Breaks the issues and/or problems into their smallest components
- Solves each component separately (i.e., maximizes the solution)
- Has no far-reaching vision or goal (just the absence of a problem)

NOTE: In Systems Thinking, the whole is primary and the parts are secondary (not vice-versa).

"If you don't know where you're going, any road will get you there."

Why Thinking Matters
"How you think... is how you act... is how you are."

Use this template to assess and analyze all your projects and issues – It is universal in its application.

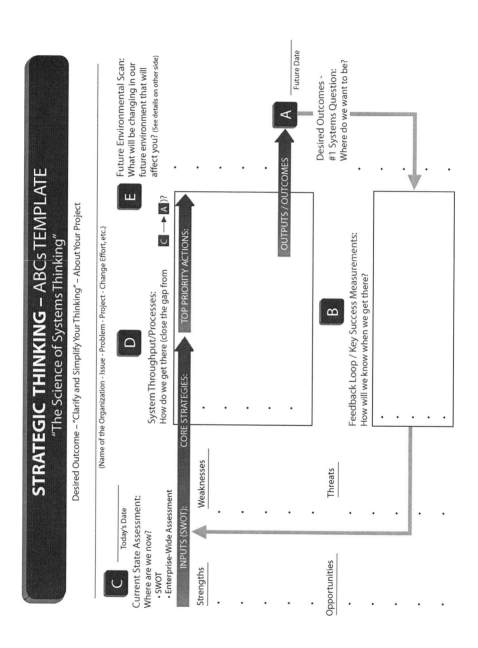

Seven Levels of Living Systems

In addition to our A-B-C Framework and definition of "systems," James G. Miller contributed a second essential concept about living systems by identifying seven levels of systems in his classic book Living Systems. These seven different levels of living (or open) systems include:

1. Single Cell (the cells that make up our physical bodies)
2. Organ (lungs, heart, kidneys)
3. Organism (humans, animals, fish, birds)
4. Group (teams, departments, strategic business units)
5. Organization (private, public, not-for-profit)
6. Society (German, Chinese, American, Indian) or Community (defined in various ways)
7. Supranational system (the earth)

Most organizations ignore the essential lesson of these seven levels of different living systems. They demonstrate that each system impacts every other system and that there is a hierarchy of systems within systems. What is a system, department, or category to you, is only a piece of an organizational system. The seven levels also illustrate the single most important feature of any system: its performance as a whole is affected by the interaction of every one of its parts. When viewed from an organizational perspective, the concept of a systems framework constitutes a total reinvention of how we think and do business. It literally creates an environment in which all processes, departments, business units, programs and subsystems are linked together to achieve the overall organizational system's outcomes (or vision).

Later on you will see how, from a practical point of view, we use these seven levels of open systems as a "Cascade of Planning" to tie the entire organization and all business units, functions, and departments together. One way to view your organization is to consider at least three levels of systems – individual, group (department, program, function, or business unit), and organization – which requires you to "cascade" your planning and change down through each level. It is the only way your strategic management system can continue to move the plan forward and perpetuate its success. Thus, as you will later see in detail "Strategic Planning" and "Business Planning" (if it exists in your organization) are really one in the same process. It is just that the Business Plan must take the Strategic Plan into consideration as the key starting point and framework to work within.

Three-Year Business Planning

"Systems are sets of components that work together for the overall objective of the whole."

The Three-Year Business Planning Process answers the question of how core strategies are to be implemented by the different organizational parts. To do this, Strategic Business Units (SBUs), Major Program Areas (MPAs), or Major Functional Areas (MFAs) that make up the organization's overall business portfolio must be identified and planned for in a multi-year timeframe, based on their importance to the organization's future growth, profitability, and direction. SBUs may be developed for any number of reasons. (See the next page for some of these reasons.)

Each Strategic Business Unit, Major Program Area, and Major Functional Area must develop concrete three-year Business Plans to carry out the core overall strategies of the larger organization. In addition, Business Plans for the "major support departments" (i.e., Human Resources, Marketing, Finance) are also crucial to ensure proper support for the business units.

The heart of our Three-Year Business Planning Process is the A-B-C-D-E Phases in the Systems Model.

Timing of Business Planning:

#1 Because annual budgeting occurs at a certain time of the year, we often see Three-Year Business Planning delayed for about 3-6 months so that the Strategic Plan/Annual Plans and Budget can be completed first. This is not optimal, but understandable.

#2 We sometimes see Three-Year Business Plans developed first, even before the organization's Strategic Plan as the Business Unit manager sees the need first. It frequently becomes "the model" for the whole organization later.

Thus, a "Cascade of Planning" down through all levels is crucial in translating the corporate strategic plan into meaningful business units and annual work plans. This is the real meaning of empowerment: strategic consistency yet operational flexibility!

Example: Giant Industries, a regional energy company, had five differ-ent business units and MFAs conduct Three-Year Business Plans once their corporate plan was completed. The impact was (15 x 5) 75 execu-tives and middle managers now fully committed to implementing their Strategic and Three-Year Business Plans.

LOBs/SBUs/MPAs/MFAs Explained

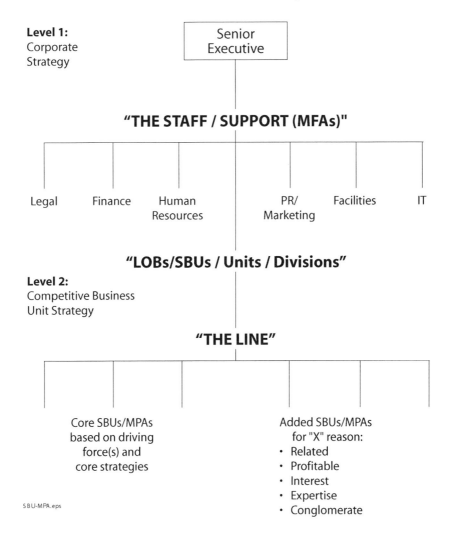

Level 1:
Corporate
Strategy

Senior
Executive

"THE STAFF / SUPPORT (MFAs)"

Legal   Finance   Human   PR/   Facilities   IT
                           Resources   Marketing

"LOBs/SBUs / Units / Divisions"

Level 2:
Competitive Business
Unit Strategy

"THE LINE"

Core SBUs/MPAs   Added SBUs/MPAs
based on driving   for "X" reason:
force(s) and   • Related
core strategies   • Profitable
                            • Interest
                            • Expertise
SBU-MPA.eps   • Conglomerate

Failing to follow this Cascade of Planning is where most organizations go wrong. They have separate department objectives and individual Key Results Areas instead of using the Corporate Core Strategies as the framework for every department's goals and each individual's performance contribution to the overall Plan.

This explicit Core Strategies link between the levels of the organization is the best way we have ever seen to make this link, integration and leverage.

Not ensuring this link between levels of the organization is one of the three things organizations most often do wrong in implementing Strategic and Business Plans successfully.

Cascade of Planning: Shared Strategies

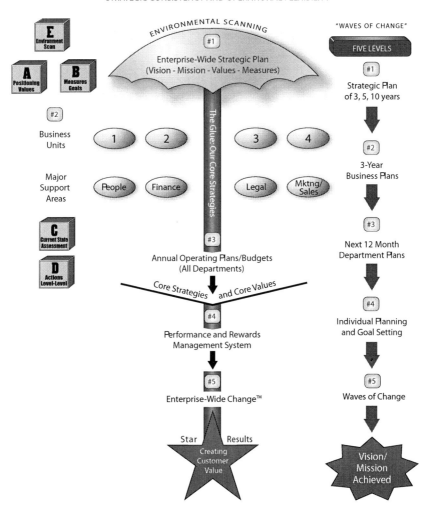

As a result of all of this chapter's thoughts, there are a whole series of "mistakes" made in Strategic Management (Strategic Thinking, Business Planning and Change Management) and "benefits" to be had under our Systems Thinking Approach°.

The 16 Common Mistakes in this A-B-C Business Planning Process:

1. Failing to integrate planning at all levels (organization-business unit-department-individual)
2. Keeping planning separate from day-to-day management
3. Conducting long-range forecasting only
4. Having a scattershot vs. systems approach to Business Planning
5. Developing only vision, mission, and value statements as fluff
6. Having yearly weekend retreats only as planning events
7. Failing to complete an effective implementation and change process
8. Violating the "people support what they help create" premise
9. Conducting business as usual after Business Planning
10. Failing to make the "tough choices," and resolving conflicts over direction
11. Lacking a scoreboard; measuring what is easy; not what is important
12. Failing to define and plan for Major Program Areas and Major Support Departments in an accurate and meaningful way within the overall organization-wide context
13. Neglecting to benchmark yourself against the competition
14. Seeing the planning document as an end in itself
15. Having confusing terminology and language
16. Trying to facilitate the process yourself instead of relying on professional facilitation and support

Which 3-6 of these 16 common mistakes might you fall victim to? Are you joining the 75% of all major changes that fail? List them here and watch out to ensure that you transcend them.

1. _____   4. _____

2. _____   5. _____

3. _____   6. _____

Benefits of the A-B-C Strategic Process

Our clients report many advantages of implementing our five-phased Three-Year Business Planning and Change Processes. As you read this list, Put a check by the ones you want:

_____ 1. This process is a proactive adaptation to a changing global world, and turbulent marketplace. It allows a firm to improve their competitive advantage(s) vs. the competition by a thorough analysis of Key Success Measures/Goals, environmental influences, and core strategies.

_____ 2. This process provides a visionary leadership process, communicating core values and strategies, so everyone can "get on the same wavelength" and align themselves to the same end: the customer. It empowers employees, teams and departments, and reduces conflict, thus making decisions easier.

_____ 3. This process enables the executive team to learn to function as a highly effective team in support of the Business Plan. This modeling of cross-functional teamwork is key to successful implementation.

_____ 4. This process is an intense executive development process for a new manager, executive, or union leader.

_____ 5. This process enables the Business Unit to develop a focused set of strategic-specific and quantifiable outcome measures of success (including financial, employee, operational, and customer satisfaction). These become the measures of success, year after year, for the organization as a whole, and for business units as they accomplish their part.

_____ 6. This process enables organizational-wide focus and priority setting to determine precision budget reallocation during tough economic times.

_____ 7. This process involves key stakeholders and employees to help create the unit's future, rather than these individuals being overwhelmed by the uncertainties of change.

_____ 8. This process enables executives and employees alike to make sense out of the confusion resulting from so many different solutions coming from the proliferation of management writers today (i.e. Six Sigma, Knowledge Management, Balanced Scorecard, Good to Great, Appreciative Inquiry, etc.)

We can add a time dimension to the five A-B-C Phased Strategic Management System. In fact, the steps constitute a circle or "Yearly Strategic Management System Cycle," which is what it really is. The model below visually depicts what we've been discussing.

If you look at the Yearly Cycle which Jack Welch used to increase shareholder value over 65 times at GE, it's simply an adaptation of this yearly cycle.

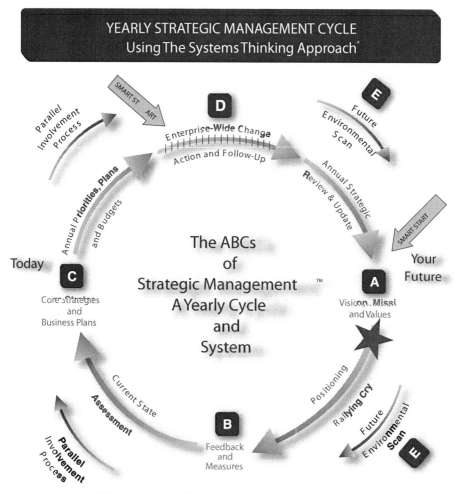

YEARLY STRATEGIC MANAGEMENT CYCLE
Using The Systems Thinking Approach

"Thinking Backwards to the Future"

CHAPTER 2
Three Main Premises

It is most important for you to understand the Three Main Premises that form the basis for our Systems Thinking Approach°. Our goal is to transform and reinvent strategic planning from its checkered past. The fact is, the number of strategic planner jobs in organizations has decreased rapidly today. Planners have become an endangered species. Planning itself, however, has increased as executives try to make sense out of today's turbulent and revolutionary times. Hence, the need to reinvent planning with these three Main Premises below has enormous implications for Business Units, Major Program Areas and Staff Functions. The Systems Thinking Approach° provides some very clear STRATEGIC ANSWERS to becoming a successful organization over the long-term. However, there is no single answer and holy grail to be found, not even the emphasis on Total Quality Management (TQM) or its successors, Business Reengineering, value chain management, Six Sigma, or any other single management fad.

The closest we will come to a holy grail is to begin with Three Main Premises, then find three possible strategic answers to each.

Main Premise #1:

"Planning and Change are the Primary Job of Leaders"

Main Premise #2:

"People Support What They Help Create"

Main Premise #3:

"Use Systems Thinking" – Focus on Outcomes: The Customer

Main Premise #1:

"Planning and Change are the Primary Job of Leaders"

A Business Unit, Department, Program, or Team embarking on a Three-Year Business Planning and Change Process must first ask itself this question: Is planning:

(1)   an event?
(2)   a process?
(3)   a change in our roles? -or-
(4)   a change in the way we run our business day-to-day?

The complete answer is "all of the above." However, Business Planning must be transformed into a system of managing strategically, and culminate in a significant change in the way business and our roles are conducted day-to-day.

This is a key difference between our model and most others which tend to suffer the fatal "SPOTS" Syndrome Strategic Business Plans On Top Shelves – gathering dust. This is actually Strategic Answer #1: achieving our three goals through installing a yearly Strategic Management Cycle and System. Business Plans are the blueprints; senior managers and department heads must change the behaviors of themselves first, then others to fill in the implementation details; based on a strategic perspective and system.

Our model is focused on the arduous implementation of real change–a change in all the diverse human behaviors that collectively make up an organization's culture. To change human behavior to a customer-focus for a Business Unit, Program, or Function, requires continual reinforcement of new behaviors. You must counter the natural human tendency to repeat familiar behaviors and habits of the past that no longer fit in the 21st century.

Thus, it cannot be stressed too early that Business Planning and the implementation/change processes must be championed over the long haul by a "monomaniac with a mission"; that champion must be the division/department top executive.

True strategic success requires a willingness to completely revamp your current management system into "a new way to run your business day-to-day." Our Business Planning Model implements numerous key concepts not found collectively in any other Business Planning and Strategic Change models, as you will see.

Goal # 1:

Developing Your Business Plan and Document:

Begin with Plan-To-Plan (Step 1)

Our "plan-to-plan" Step #1 concept educates, assesses, organizes, and tailors the business planning process to the unit's specific needs. It involves key stakeholders in the "Parallel Involvement Process" concept as well as clarifying top executive roles in leading, developing and owning their Plan. This is a one-day, introductory session, with a Nothing-to-Lose Guarantee and No Further Obligation (something all consultants should offer you). Only if the session is successful in the view of both parties should you go ahead.

If You Go Ahead: Conduct Actual Three-Year Business Planning Phases E-A-B-C)

After the Plan-to-Plan, you conduct the Three-Year Business Planning. The concept of an "Ideal Future Vision" is the starting point for Strategic Thinking and a Strategic Management Process – a clear, shared "Ideal Future Vision" that helps clarify and implement tough choices. It focuses the organization and its core strategies on satisfying the customer; your only outcome (or reason for existence).

At the same time, you need to conduct a Future Environmental Scan of the trends for the next three years and beyond.

Steps #2 - #5, shown on the next page, help you see the blueprint or strategic design. You will also include the development of organizational values or "culture," the measurement of quantifiable outcome measures, goals, or Key Success Measures/Goals.

Lastly, you will develop a Current State Assessment, and then the core strategies are developed to "fill the gap" between the Vision of the Future and today's assessment.

Conduct Annual Operational Planning (Phase C Also)

Once these Three-Year Business Plans are developed, the annual plans and strategic budgets, tied to the annual actions and priorities, must be set. Annual plans and budgets must be set within the context of the core strategies already developed. To set separate department objectives is a big mis-

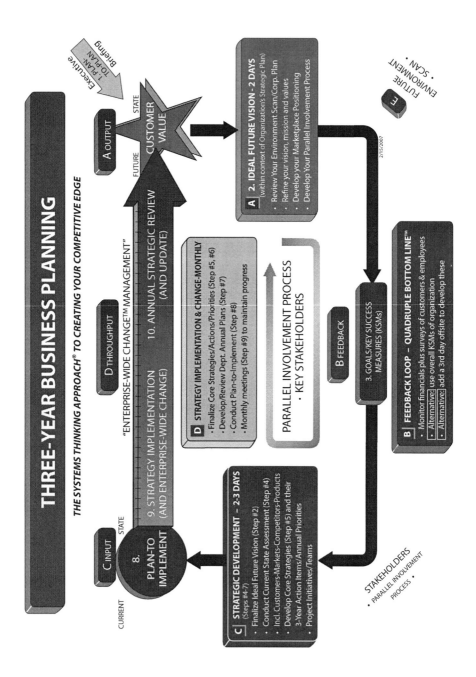

THREE-YEAR BUSINESS PLANNING

THE SYSTEMS THINKING APPROACH® TO CREATING YOUR COMPETITIVE EDGE

1. PLAN-TO-PLAN Executive Briefing

A OUTPUT

CUSTOMER VALUE

FUTURE STATE

D THROUGHPUT

"ENTERPRISE-WIDE CHANGE™ MANAGEMENT"

9. STRATEGY IMPLEMENTATION (AND ENTERPRISE-WIDE CHANGE)

10. ANNUAL STRATEGIC REVIEW (AND UPDATE)

A | 2. IDEAL FUTURE VISION - 2 DAYS
(within context of Organization's Strategic Plan)
• Review Your Environment Scan/Corp. Plan
• Refine your vision, mission and values
• Develop your Marketplace Positioning
• Develop Your Parallel Involvement Process

E FUTURE ENVIRONMENT SCAN

2/15/2007

D | STRATEGY IMPLEMENTATION & CHANGE-MONTHLY
• Finalize Core Strategies/Actions/Priorities (Step #5, #6)
• Develop/Review Dept. Annual Plans (Step #7)
• Conduct Plan-to-Implement (Step #8)
• Monthly meetings (Step #9) to maintain progress

PARALLEL INVOLVEMENT PROCESS
• KEY STAKEHOLDERS

B FEEDBACK

3. GOALS/KEY SUCCESS MEASURES (KSMs)

B | FEEDBACK LOOP – QUADRUPLE BOTTOM LINE™
• Monitor financials plus surveys of customers & employees
• Alternative: use overall KSMs of organization
• Alternative: add a 3rd day offsite to develop these

C INPUT

CURRENT STATE

8. PLAN-TO-IMPLEMENT

C | STRATEGIC DEVELOPMENT – 2-3 DAYS
(Steps #4-7)
• Finalize Ideal Future Vision (Step #2)
• Conduct Current State Assessment (Step #4)
• Incl. Customers-Markets-Competitors-Products
• Develop Core Strategies (Step #5) and their
• 3-Year Action Items/Annual Priorities
• Project Initiatives/Teams

STAKEHOLDERS
• PARALLEL INVOLVEMENT PROCESS •

take as the "Department's Objectives" of each department in every organization should be to support the Core Strategies of the overall organization.

Example: One municipality we know spent considerable time and effort on a strategic planning process. However, department planning and budgeting were completed separately without linkages to the organization's strategic planning. It didn't take long before the departments realized that they could ignore the strategic planning because of no follow up and evaluations that were not tied to it.

It is essential that all key line and staff units ultimately develop their own three year Business Plans under the umbrella of the overall strategic plan.

This need to link levels of planning into one system is a commonly missed concept and a serious omission.

Goal # 2:
Ensuring Successful Implementation and Change:

"Bridging The Gap: Plan-To-Implement"

The Plan-to-Implement (Phase D) is designed to "bridge the gap" between business planning and the difficult implementation process. It is an additional educating, assessing, organizing, and tailoring opportunity for the change effort. Key is installing supporting structures such as a Strategic Change Leadership Team, a yearly Comprehensive Map of the Implementation Process, and the use of cross-functional Strategy Project Teams. These are all part of our "Fail-Safe Mechanisms" that are embodied in Step #8 to ensure successful implementation.

This Goal #2 also includes Strategy Implementation and Change, where the actual work and tasks get accomplished. Companies that want to go beyond the simplistic techniques such as SWOT often use of our Organization as a System / Business Excellence Architecture model as the Systems Thinking Approach™ to provide simplicity to guide successful implementation and the fit and linkage of all parts of the organization to its overall Vision, Mission, and Values.

Keep in mind, you do not implement a Three-Year Business Plan, you implement an Annual Operating Plan, based on the Business Plan. The

Centre provides a free article on this Business Excellence Architecture at our website: www.HainesCentre.com.

Goal #3:
Create and Sustain High Performance – Over the Long Term

Annual Strategic Review (and Update) - Year After Year

Goal #3 includes an Annual Strategic Review and Update, much as you would include a yearly independent financial audit. Business Plans often span for three or more years, yet need formal reviews and updating yearly to keep pace with change.

Business Plans must be living and breathing documents. This is the only way to sustain High Performance over the long-term.

In summary, this Three Goal Strategic Management System and Yearly Cycle includes all the elements necessary to design and build a customer-focused high performance Business Unit/Functional Area. It will be explained in more detail throughout this book.

Main Premise #2:
"People Support What They Help Create"

An organization's first year of business planning involves setting in place the necessary planning strategies and creating a critical mass for the desired changes. A core planning team of eight to twelve people from your collective leadership should lead the process, do the hard work, and make the decisions.

Perhaps the most crucial planning team task is a "Parallel Involvement Process" (see next page's graphic) involving the rest of management (both Corporate and Your Unit) and other key stakeholders in a meaningful way; gathering their input on all draft documents and increasing their ownership of the plan. This is the second seemingly simple element; "People support what they help create."

Example: During its Plan-to-Plan step, one school district in California established a core planning team of 15 people. However, because of the district's broad impact on the lives of thousands of families, its Parallel Involvement Process with key stakeholders included over 100 meetings involving 2000+ people.

***The diagram below summarizes the process
of ensuring people support what they help create.***

PARALLEL INVOLVEMENT PROCESS
"People Support What They Help Create"

INSTEAD OF D.A.D.: Decide, Announce, Defend

SET UP THE PLANNING & CHANGE COMMUNITY

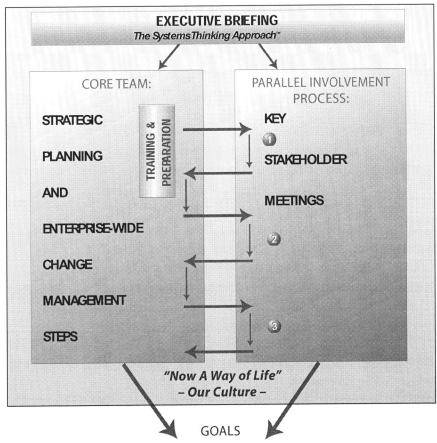

GOALS

#1 Ownership For Implementation / Execution

#2 Best Possible Decisions On Future Direction / Purpose

In these Parallel Involvement Process meetings, some key points are essential to success.

Parallel Involvement Process Meetings
Purpose (and Agenda)

1. Explain the Strategic Planning / Enterprise-Wide Change effort and your role or involvement in it.
2. Help us understand draft documents more clearly.
3. Provide input and feedback to take to the full core planning team.
   - Guarantee: Your feedback will be seriously considered.
   - Limitation: Input is being gathered from many different people.

Therefore, it is impossible for each person's input to be automatically placed in the final document exactly as desired.

Overall Meeting Purpose

1. This is an information sharing and input/feedback meeting.
2. Not a decision-making meeting. This is done by the Core Planning/ Enterprise-Wide Team at their next meeting, based on your feedback.

Premise #2 leads to Strategic Answer #2: the need for "Visionary Leadership Practices" that are different from the feared bosses of the past. Leaders at multiple levels as trainers, coaches and facilitators are needed to carry out this Parallel Involvement Process during planning and implementation. The wide range of "participative management" and leadership skills must be acquired by all personnel in managerial positions. Make sure to avoid two extremes of "Feared Bosses" and "Too Nice Bosses."

The only advantage over the long-term for any organization is its leadership.

Strategic Leadership

Employees become your greatest assets only if the leaders allow them to be. Strategic Leadership requires a number of different skills and six levels of Natural Leadership competencies.

H (High)
M (Med.)
L (Low)

What are your personal skills at each Leadership Level?

Level #1	Enhancing Your Self-Mastery	
Level #2	Building Relationships	_____
Level #3	Building Effective Teams	_____
Level #4	Building Customer-Focused Business Processes	_____
Level #5	Integrating Organizational Outcomes	_____
Level #6	Creating Value for the Customer	_____

Acquiring these skills does not happen overnight, as "leadership is a contemplative art" requiring a commitment to separate professional growth opportunity over a long period of time. The ability to lead an entire organization and all its facets and levels effectively is quite a daunting task, requiring a life-long learning perspective.

Thus, it is imperative for organizations to develop a fully comprehensive "Strategic Leadership Development System" to ensure each leader develops these six core competencies. For details on this we refer the reader to the free article on our website (www.HainesCentre.com), called "Leadership Development is Bankrupt."

Main Premise #3:

"Use Systems Thinking" to Focus on Outcomes: The Customer

The key to the Systems Thinking Approach™ is simple: to focus on your outcomes (Destination Thinking).

"Begin with the end in mind" (Stephen Covey) and think backwards to achieve your future. For all units, focusing on the most important outcome means focusing on the customer. This is STRATEGIC ANSWER #3; the need for every unit to become both 1) an outcome oriented system and 2) focused on the customer.

This common sense focus on the customer, however, is frequently not "how we are driven" as a business unit, function, or program area. Historically, organizations often start because either someone invented a "better mousetrap" (i.e., a product to sell), someone has venture capital available to invest (i.e., a profit motive), or a government grant or granted monopoly exists (i.e., a regulation orientation). They often do not focus on providing customer value.

The History of Providing Customer Value

"From order taking to zero defects, to Deming, to reengineering..."

The history of providing customer value has evolved over the past 20 years. First, during the Industrial Era, mass production and mass marketing produced products for the "average" customer. This created "order taking" behaviors. Customers selected from what was available. In the 1970s, quality control and "zero defects" attempted to refine this internally oriented process even more. In the 1980s, many of the methods made popular by the Japanese came to the U.S. (Deming, Juran, PDCA, JIT, Kaizen, etc.).

In the 1990s, cost-cutting, waste elimination, and reengineering were dominant due to cut-throat global competition. Despite their positive aspects, our research of current business trends and client assessments show that these efforts are still separate and fragmented solutions. Most firms in the 21st century still do not have regular and systematic customer feedback mechanisms, so they don't really know what their customers value.

For example: Try grading how your organization is currently driven vs. these six options by spreading a total of 10 points across all six choices:

1. Regulatory; the "why"   _____
2. Operations; the "how"   _____
3. Profits; the "why"   _____
4. Products; the "what"   _____
5. Employees; the "how"   _____
6. Customers; the "who"   _____

                               TOTAL (10 pts.)   _____

If you selected Option "6" with the most points, then see the next list to verify whether you really are driven by the 15 characteristics of Customer-Focused Organizations.

As a result of the difficult history of providing customer value, we have listed the following 15 key characteristics of successful customer-focused organizations. These "Key Commandments" are based on our best practices research in this area, and can help you assess how your organization or unit measures up. Rate each of these characteristics on a scale from 1 (Low) to 10 (High):

Customer-Focused Organizations

_____ 1. Are "close to the customer" – especially senior executives (i.e., see, touch, feel, meet and dialogue with them face-to-face on a regular basis out in the marketplace).

_____ 2. Executives – include the customers in their decisions, focus groups, meetings, planning and deliberations.

_____ 3. Know and anticipate the customers' needs, wants and desire – continually, as they change.

_____ 4. Surpassing customer needs is the driving force of the entire organization.

_____ 5. Survey the customers' satisfaction with our products and services on a regular basis.

_____ 6. Have a clear "positioning" in the marketplace vs. the competition in the eyes of the customer.

_____ 7. Focus on Creating Customer Value – i.e., "value-added" benefits to the customer. See our Star ★ Results Model (quality products and services, customer choice, responsiveness, delivery, speed, and service vs. total cost of doing business with you).

_____ 8. Set quality customer-service standards – expectations that are specific and measurable to each department.

_____ 9. Customer Service Standards are based on customer input and focus groups.

_____ 10. Require everyone in the organization to experience moments of truth by meeting and serving the customer directly – at least one day every year.

_____ 11. Focus and reengineer the business processes based on the customer needs and perceptions – and do it across functions.

_____ 12. Focus the organization structure based on the marketplace - i.e., structure the organization by customer markets (1 customer = 1 representative).

_____ 13. Reward customer-focused behaviors (especially cross-functional teams that work together to serve customers).

_____ 14. Have a clear policy, and a widespread use of recovery strategies to surpass customer expectations.

_____ 15. Hire and promote "customer friendly" people.

In Summary

When you use these 15 characteristics of a customer-focused organization, is becomes obvious that satisfying your customer's needs and wants should be the primary focus of your "organization as a system" (versus becoming enslaved by obsolete activities as ends in themselves). This is especially important for Public Sector and Not-For-Profit organizations who do not have the profit motive to keep them fo cused on the customer and on outputs.

Thus, the focus of this Business Planning Guide is our Customer-Focused, Strategic Management A-B-C-D-E Systems Model, which has been reinvented for the 21st Century based on:

1. Customer needs and desired outcomes
2. Extensive research in General Systems Theory
3. The three authors' experiences as a CEO, as executives, and as consultants for over 80 years total
4. Constant practical application and refinements from our clients

Most importantly, however, is that it is the result of a comprehensive literature search and a comparative analysis of 14 other popular strategic planning models. Yet, the most disturbing elements missing from all of these 14 models reviewed was both (1) our Systems Thinking Approach™ based on the science of General Systems Theory and (2) lack of focus on the customer outcomes as the primary purpose of all enterprises, Business Units, and Major Function Areas (MFAs).

As we've said, the best way to describe any "system" is with a series of $\boxed{C}$ Inputs to a $\boxed{D}$ Process or Throughput that creates value added $\boxed{A}$ Outputs into the $\boxed{E}$ External Environment that the Customer will buy, use, desire and appreciate. Those four characteristics along with a fifth, $\boxed{B}$ Feedback Loop, comprise the main components of General Systems Theory (GST); the most basic way to look at any living system and the Natural Way the World Works.

Many A-B-C-D-E Applications

There are many variations of the A-B-C-D-E Five Phases of Strategic Management System we have developed and used with specific units/functions. The models are attached here and can be accessed at www.Systems-ThinkingPress.com along with free 4-page articles about them. Some are attached in our Appendix, if you want more details.

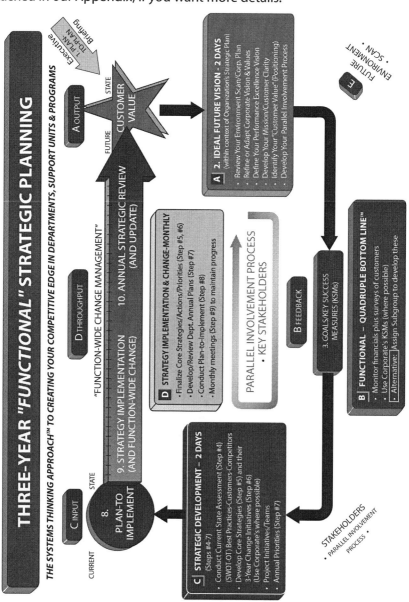

CHAPTER 3
Step #1: Executive Briefing and Plan-to-Plan Day

This step is essential. We will not contract for Business Planning before this innovative step is conducted as a one-day "Executive Briefing" and "Plan-to-Plan Day" for CEOs, Executive Directors and top executives. This briefing ensures that everyone has the same foundation in our Business Planning model and terminology. It ensures the joint tailoring and crafting of a Business Planning process that makes sense to the executives and to the consultant. Even if a Business Planning process is not pursued, this Executive Briefing and Plan-to-Plan examination is valuable and informative in its own right as a unique diagnostic and learning opportunity.

Numerous strategic issues are identified and discussed in this step. In addition, environmental scanning and project organizing tasks are pursued. Thus, we call this step an "Educating, Assessing, Organizing and Tailoring" day. It is also where you come face-to-face with the need to upgrade your collective leadership skills to successfully implement your plans.

This session also usually includes defining issues such as personal readiness and commitment, barriers to success, planning team membership, staff support roles and key stakeholder involvement.

Roles of Staff Support and External Consultants

To ensure successful planning and implementation, a Business Unit, Program or Function usually needs an external consultant to facilitate the process and deal with difficult executive and strategic issues. The external consultant must also work with an internal consultant and support cadre who will develop their skills to the point that they can carry on the process mostly without the consultant. Until that time, the consultant fulfills the role of a neutral facilitator and devil's advocate, with the abilities of a strategist as well as handling conflicting ideas and issues that arise in the core planning team's deliberations.

Human resistance to change is substantial; longtime organizational members tend to support the status quo. This is also true for many senior executives, who have substantial power and authority, and the most to lose in change. Our motto in these intense and difficult planning sessions is "If things are going smoothly, we must be doing something wrong."

Keep in mind that Business Planning, as well as the management of change, is a disciplined, scientific endeavor in which organizations have rarely made a significant internal investment in the necessary knowledge or skills. Business schools and universities have not included this subject in their curricula until recently. Thus, most of us have learned about planning and change via on-the-job role models who either preserved the inadequate status quo, instituted incremental change, or haphazardly coped with "seat of the pants" strategic change.

As a strategist, facilitator, and devil's advocate, the external consultant helps the executives and the core planning team to:

- Have a specific and proven planning process based on the Systems Thinking Approach™
- Facilitate the planning process without taking over its direction
- Act consistently with their desired values in the planning process
- Develop their own concrete decisions, directions, and priorities
- Confront the issues whenever backsliding occurs
- Keep their focus on Best Practices Research as a "devil's advocate"
- Develop internal consultants/support cadre to take over the process
- They must be a cheerleader who exemplifies and promotes a primary faith in people, their vision, and will to achieve

To see the full range of possible "Staff Support" needed for a successful planning and implementation process, see the following matrix:

Business Planning "Staff Support Team" Functions

List Staff Support Team Names:

Position	Typical Tasks	Name
1. Planning	• Business Planning • Annual Planning • Current State Assessment _____	
2. Finance	• Key Success Measure Coordinator • Budgeting • Current State Assessment	
3. Human Resources	• Performance/Rewards Management • Training and Development	
4. Communications	• Updates after each Meeting • Print Final Plan/Plaques • Rollout Plan	
5. Administrative Assistant	• Logistics/Follow-up • Laptop Minutes/Document Revisions • Drafts Business Plan	
6. Internal Coordinator Coordinates or performs items 1-7 themselves	**Minimum List** • Parallel Involvement Process • Internal Facilitator • Coordinates Entire Process • Teach Organization About This _____	
7. External Consultant	• Facilitates Planning Team • Develops Internal Coordinator • Devil's Advocate/Tough Choices • Advisor on all Planning/Change • Facilitates the Change Leadership Team _____	

Tailored to Your Needs

Finally, after the educational briefing component in the morning, the Plan-to-Plan afternoon allows you to organize and tailor the process to your unique needs. Tailoring issues include linking to your annual planning and budgeting time frames and the need for a strategic change management process once planning is complete. See our Appendix for a format/exercise we use to do this.

This last commitment involves developing a new way to run your business as a Customer-Focused organization via our Three Goal Strategic Management Systems' Solution. It is vital to understand this BEFORE you begin as you usually have only one credible shot at doing Business Planning successfully.

In summary, this Plan-to-Plan step and all its tasks (see chart of additional ones) are vital to "educate, assess, organize, and tailor" yourself before you begin the actual Business Planning. Learning to "clarify and simplify" everything we do is key in designing and building our customer-focused high performance organization.

Potential Plan-to-Plan Tasks to
Educate, Assess, Tailor, and Organize the Process to Your Needs

EDUCATE

1. Organization Specification Sheet

2. Executive Briefing on Business Planning

3. Organizational Fact Sheet for Business Planning

4. Individual Commitment to Strategic Management Must Be High (not just to Business Planning)

5. Organizational Commitment to a Strategic Management System/ Yearly Cycle (Planning-People-Leadership-Change)

ORGANIZE

1. Business Planning "Staff Support Team" Needed

2. Identification of Key Stakeholders

3. Planning Team Membership Selected

4. Key Stakeholder Involvement

5. Business Planning Meeting (Process Observer for Team Building)

6. Action/"To Do" List, Minutes (Format to use)

7. Meeting Processing (Guide to Use)

8. Meeting Closure – Action Planning Checklist (at the end of each meeting)

ASSESS

1. A High-Performance Best Practices Organizational Assessment (Building on Baldrige)

2. Pre-work Business Planning Briefing Questionnaire

3. Personal Readiness/Experiences in Business Planning

4. Business Planning Process (past Levels of Effectiveness/Simplicity Audit)

5. Readiness Steps and Actions (Barriers and Issues)

6. Critical Issues List

7. Initial Environmental Scanning required

TAILOR

1. Tailored to Your Needs: of the Reinventing Business Planning Model

2. Business Planning Links: (to Corporate Strategic Plan, Annual Budgets, Department Plans)

3. Leadership Development Skills (Organizational and Individual Self-Change/Training Needed)

4. Business Planning Updates Communicated to Others

5. Learning possibilities during Business Planning

6. Enterprise-Wide Change Process: Smart Start and Plan-to-Plan Implement Scheduled

75% Of All Major Change Efforts Fail

In Summary

The need for a one-day Plan-to-Plan Day is essential to a "Smart Start" that helps to engineer the success of your Three-Year Business Planning up front. A failure to do so is why our 2005 research on Enterprise-Wide Change shows that 75% of all major changes fail to achieve their Goals/Vision.

Hence, the vital importance of the Plan-to-Plan Day, with the:

A.M. - Educating and Assessing

P.M. - Organizing and Tailoring

... the Planning Process

CHAPTER 4
Phase E: Future Environmental Scan

"The only limits, as always, are those of vision."

– Eleanor Roosevelt

Part of Step #1 is to conduct a Future Environmental Scan using our SKEPTIC framework (Socio-Demographics, Kompetition, Economics/ Ecology, Political, Technical, Industry/substitutes, Customer). You become a futurist to ensure your plan is not developed in a vacuum. Involvement of staff in doing this results in a richer scan to guide your Three-Year Business Planning.

This scan ensures that everyone has the same foundation with regard to our Reinventing Strategic Management (Planning-People-Leadership Change) model and terminology.

Once the Environmental Scan is completed, then the ABCs of Strategic Planning and Change begin in earnest. However, first we need to complete this Future Environmental Scan.

We are in the era of revolutionary change. It is fundamental, radical, and global. These are incredible times of transformation typified by high growth and market opportunity; worldwide expansion and competition; corporate mergers, acquisitions, and other restructurings; and downsizing, obsolescence, and unforeseen events representing a shift in the business paradigm.

What are the implications of all this revolutionary change?

Action: Scan the environment around your own Business Unit.

Environmental Trends

What are the environmental trends – projections – opportunities – threats facing us over the life of our Business Plan?

Action: Start brainstorming here:

1.

2.

3.

4.

5.

6.

7.

8.

9.

10.

Action: Now, use the SKEPTIC Framework on the next page to be Systemic and Comprehensive about your Future Scan.

The SKEPTIC form provides a way of organizing and understanding elements in your business environment – current and future – that can enhance or threaten your potential success.

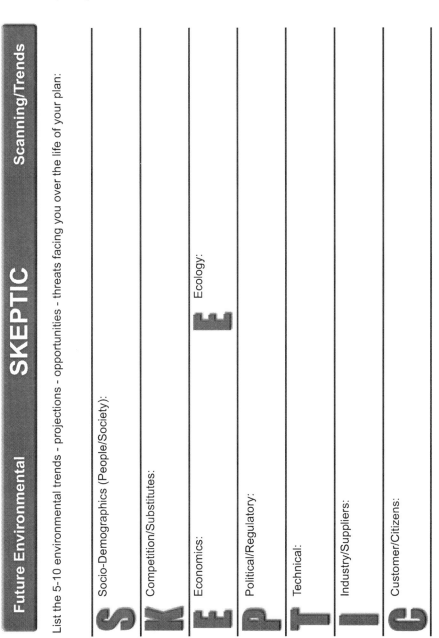

For instance, here is some scanning to consider:

Socio Demographics (People/Society)

1. World Wide English Culture (MTV - CNN - BBC)
2. Indonesia - Long Term Play
3. USA Sinking to First World - Third World - Society Breakdown

K or C: Competition/Substitutes

1. Three Language Skills – World Intelligence Levels
2. Multilateralism – Cooperation – Asia
3. Future Emerging Global Markets
4. Increasing and Global Competition-Substitutes

Economics

1. Hybrid Cars – Oil Dependency
2. Deficit – Dollar Value – China Purchasing of Treasuries
3. Global Labor Arbitrage – India Today – Outsourcing
4. Internet Impact - Changing Rules

Ecological

1. Environmental Movement – China
2. Kyoto Treaty in Effect World-Wide: USA Isolated
3. Global Warming Reality
4. World-Wide Water Quality and Fights

Political – Regulatory

1. First World - Third World – Persistent Poverty Still
2. Global War on Terrorism
3. WTO Decisions
4. OIC – OPEC – Oil/Energy

Technology

1. 250,000 Engineering Graduates/Year in India
2. China Graduates 5x the USA Number Each Year
3. Biotech Revolution Just Beginning
4. Global Internet Impact – New Rules
5. Technology Integration A Big Issue – Open vs. Closed:

Strategic and Systems Thinking vs. Analytic Thinking

Industry – Suppliers

1. Global Raw Materials Shortage - Sucking Sound:
   China - India
2. Transnational Companies/Culture vs. Countries
3. Every industry has a new Dynamics - Challenges - Rules
4. Global Sourcing

Customers – Clients (Citizens)

1. Customers want it all – Good – Fast – and Cheap (especially cheap)
2. Customers are much more demanding – Low Loyalty
3. Pendulum has swung to Consumer Power
4. Gen 'Y' Power – Boomers and Gen 'X' less important

In Sum... Staying Ahead of Global Trends
Rate of Change in the World

"If the rate of change on the outside exceeds the rate of change on the inside, the end is near."

– Jack Welch
Former Chairman and CEO
General Electric Corporation

Levels of Future Environmental Scanning
SKEPTIC System Levels

8 – The World/Earth

7 – The Region/Continent – North America/Etc.

6 – USA/Country

5 – Government/Society/Community

4 – Company/Organization

3 – Dept./Function

2 – Project/Team

1 – Me (and You)

2006 Some Fascinating Trends

1. Global War on Terrorism
2. Hybrid Card – Oil Dependency
3. Three Language Skills – World Intelligence Levels Climbing
4. World-Wide Culture (MTV-English)
5. Global Labor Market-Transnational Culture vs. Countries Anymore
6. Multilateralism – Asian Alliances
7. Environmental Movement – China
8. Indonesia and Brazil – Long Term/Future Players
9. Iraq War - By-Products (Settling Disputes - Freedoms)
10. First World - Third World – Persistent Poverty Still in China/India
11. USA Sinking to First World - Third World - Society Breakdown
12. World-Wide Raw Materials Shortage – Sucking Sound of China-India

New Challenges and Strategic Opportunities of the 21st Century
Examples of Past Paradigm Shifts

1. Environmental Mainstream vs. Extremists

2. Swiss Watches vs. Quartz/Digital

3. Made in Japan Quality vs. Cheap

4. 77 mpg Car vs. Gas Guzzlers

5. Solar/Methane Cars vs. Oil

6. PCs vs. Mainframe Computers

7. Xerox Copy vs. Carbon Copy-CC

8. Fax vs. Mail

9. Express Mail vs. Snail Mail

10. Wires vs.Wireless

11. Cellular/Airfone vs. Telephone

12. Airplanes vs. Drones

13. Electrical vs. Electronics/Internet

14. DVDs and CDs vs. Plastic

15. Fall of Berlin Wall vs. USSR

16. Mass Customization/Robotics vs. Any Color – Black (H. Ford)

17. Global Village vs. National Economy

18. Flexible Work Hours vs. Standard 9-5 Hours

19. Electronics/Cottage Industry – Free Agent Nation vs. Big Firms

20. What is next in your business? (see next page)

Systems Thinking Paradigm Shifts

Obsolescence

...as a result of the current paradigm shift, the standard way of doing business is rapidly becoming obsolete and irrelevant.

Old-Fashioned Industrial Age Concepts	New Systems Age Concepts
Bureaucracy/Functions	Network and Integration
Focus on Institution	Focus on Individuals/Teams
Control	Empowerment
Structure	Flexibility/Minimum Hierarchy
Stability	Change
Self-Sufficiency	Interdependencies
Directive Management	Inspirational Leadership/Vision
Affordable Quality	Shared
Personal Security	Value-Added
Title, Rank, Compensation	Personal Growth
To Compete	Making a Difference
Domestic	To Build and Sustain
Vertical Integration	Global/World Village
Economy of Scale	Alliances/Collaborations
Single Loop Learning	Economy of Speed
	Double-Loop Learning

Future Emerging Global Markets

1. Argentina, Chile, and Mercusor
2. Brazil
3. China
4. Germany and EU
5. India
6. Indonesia
7. Mexico and Central America
8. Malaysia
9. South and East Africa
10. South Korea

China

1. Manufacturing center for the world
2. Raw materials demands
3. Currency level
4. USA investments/Tied to our economy
5. Non English speaking generally
6. Local elections
7. Mekong River Dam - Environmentalists win
8. Taiwan

India

1. India – 3 Times the population & one-third the size of the USA
2. Political Elections – Still proceed with modernization – a human face
3. British Legacy: Rule of Law and Bureaucracy-
4. People: 2/3rds still in poverty-rural India (First World-Third World)
5. Outsourcing: Software-Call Centers-Pharmaceuticals (Drs.)
6. People: English-International-Bright-Hard Working-USA trained
7. People: 250,000 engineering graduates a year (Education key)
8. People Demand: Retention issues-going to older people

What is its place as a world leader in 30+ years?

Developing a Strategic Environmental Scanning System
The Six Steps Include the Following:

1. Identify the organization's Environmental Scan needs, especially for the next round of Strategic Planning (Annual Updates).
2. Generate a list of information sources that provide core inputs (i.e., trade shows, publications, technical meetings, customers, shareholders).
3. Identify those employees who will participate in the Environmental Scanning Process. (Not just members of the Planning Team.)
4. Assign scanning tasks for each SKEPTIC letter to several members of the organization.
5. Collect data on a regular basis.
6. Disseminate the information in a large group meeting:
   • on yearly and quarterly basis at a Change Leadership Team meeting.

Initial Environmental Scan

Based on your initial environmental scanning, do you need to collect any further information or scan again?

Instructions: List any additional initial environmental scanning that needs to be conducted at the beginning of the strategic planning process.

To Do List

What to collect?	Who?	By when?

To deal with these radical changes in our lives and careers, we must honestly join this transformation, since there is no resisting it. It is a time for new visions, strategies, programs, and actions – revolution, not evolution.

Implications: Critical Issues List

As a final task...

Action: In order to ground your planning process, complete the following task:

What are the 5-10 most important critical issues facing us today as an organization?

1.

2.

3.

4.

5.

6.

7.

8.

9.

10.

Note: Keep this list in mind throughout the planning process, to keep the focus on real issues.

NOTES:

CHAPTER 5
Phase A: Ideal Future Vision

"The only limits, as always, are those of Vision"

STEP #2: Ideal Future Vision

This Step is concerned with formulating dreams that are worth believing in and fighting for. At this stage in beginning the actual Business Planning process, the cry of "It cannot be done!" is irrelevant; how to turn it into reality is pursued after the vision is created. It is about creating your own future!

Four challenges are met during this step:

Challenge #1 To conduct a visioning process to develop a shared Vision Statement of your dreams, hopes, and desired image of your future.

Note: If your overall company/organization has a Vision, it is normal to reaffirm and adapt it rather than develop a separate one. We recommend one overall organization equals one Vision.

Challenge #2 To develop a Mission Statement describing why your Business Unit, MPA, or Function exists, what business it is in, and who it serves. Becoming a customer-focused organization begins here with a clear definition of who your customers are. (See later page on the "Mission Development Triangle Exercise.")

Note: Each Unit needs its own mission because its customers and products/services are usually unique and must be clearly articulated.

Challenge #3 To articulate Core Values that guide day-to-day behavior and collectively create your desired culture. (See later page on the "Organizational Values Exercise.")

Note: If your overall company organization has a set of Core Values, it is normal to reaffirm and adapt them rather than develop a new set. Each unit must adopt the organization's values, however, some units have added one or two additional values that describe how they behave.

Challenge #4 To discuss the need for a Rallying Cry – a crisp and concise (8 words or less) statement of the entire Business Plan and its Customer-Focus.

Note: If your overall company organization has a currently meaningful Rallying Cry, it is normal to reaffirm and adapt it rather than develop a new set.

To better understand these four challenges of Step #2 – see the following definitions of this Ideal Future Step.

Ideal Future Step #2

1. Vision: Aspirational – Idealistic   ***"Our Guiding Star"***
   - Our view/image of what the ideal future looks like at time "X"
   - It has dreamlike qualities, future hopes and aspirations, even if they are never fully attainable
   - An energizing, positive, and inspiring statement of where and what we want to be in the future
2. Mission: Pragmatic – Realistic ***"Our Unique Purpose"***
   - What business are we in? (not the activities we do)
   - "Why we exist – our reason for being"
   - The purpose towards which we commit our work life
   - What we produce; its benefits/outcomes
   - Who we serve – our customers/clients
3. Core Values: Our Beliefs – ***"What We Believe In"***
   - How do we, or should we act while accomplishing this business or mission?
   - "The way we do our business" – our process
   - Principles that guide our daily behaviors
   - What we believe in and how we will act at work
4. Positioning: Our Driving Force - Distinctiveness ***"Our Competitive Edge"***
   - Grand strategy–strategy–strategic intent–competitive advantage
   - What positions us uniquely in the marketplace that causes the customer to do business with us – Customer Value
5. Rallying Cry: Our Essence - Motivational Force ***"Our Memorizable Essence"***
   - A crisp slogan (8 words or less) easily remembered by employees, representing the essence of the vision, mission, and core values (i.e., the driving force/positioning upon which all else revolves)
   - It should be a powerful motivational force that's memorable, memorizable, believable, repeatable, and lived on a daily basis across the organization – everywhere and in every way.

In today's dynamic environment of global competition and rapid technological growth and obsolescence, changing an organization to become more "Customer-Focused" is extremely difficult. This is especially true for organizations that have been successful in the past through a product-driven or technological orientation, or by public institutions that enjoyed monopolies or protective government mandates. Deregulation, outsourcing, and global competition of all sorts has forced organizations to become "Customer Focused" in order to survive. Focusing on your customer, their wants and needs, is fast becoming the last true competitive advantage for organizations. Quality products have become the de-facto price of admission for entering an industry, not a competitive edge.

Understanding Positioning
The Customer must now become the focus!

This need for change has led senior executives in both the public and private sectors worldwide to the perplexing quandary of how to find the formula for future success. This "formula" is called Positioning. The proliferation of management writings, since Tom Peter's In Search Of Excellence, has only added to this quandary. Many of these writers promise the ONE Holy Grail that will solve all of management's problems. Even TQM, despite its obvious logical importance, is taking a beating in the literature. So how is one to sort out all the management writings and Fads of today? Is it now Business Process Re-Engineering or Value Change Management that we need and not TQM? What about Six Sigma, Empowerment, or Leadership or Teamwork or Service Management, or _____ (you fill in the blank).

"In every instance, we found that the best run companies stay as close to their customers as is humanly possible" (Tom Peters, et. al.)

Fortunately, there is a way to make sense of all these writings and fads; and at the same time, create a Customer-Focused Organization. These organizations have a clear Positioning in the marketplace in the eyes of their customers vs. the competition that causes them to do business with you.

It is obvious to some of the smartest companies around that the customer is #1 and that all else should flow from the customer. Southwest Airlines, Nordstroms, Marriott, and Toyota are just a few Customer Focused organizations. However, getting to their level of focus and positioning usually requires a J. W. Marriott, a Herb Kelleher or else a Systems Thinking

Framework in which to get the entire organizations thinking AND acting in support of the customer and your positioning. Actually both our Systems Thinking Approach™ Framework and J.W. Marriott would be the ideal. However, lacking a J.W. Marriott-type leader in charge over a long period of time, we can still create a "Customer-Focused" organization by using a Systems Framework to clarify and simplify our Positioning.

This Systems Framework can help us understand, make sense of, and even unite the business plans and major changes any organization can undertake.

We have a strong bias that the place to begin using this Systems Thinking Framework is through understanding that customers have "multiple outcomes" they desire from any organization just as every system has multiple options. Our extensive research has shown that the range of potential customer wants and needs is a combination of five potential results, which we call World Class Star ★ Results (see following page on this Star). Knowing your customer wants a mix of these five points on the Star gives you a better place to begin to "Create Customer Value" and position your organization/business unit (where the real, true competition is) versus the competition in the private sector.

Use this star as a final check on whether your Vision and Mission are specific and complete regarding who the customer is and what they value.

Two Key Questions Here:

#1 What is the one thing on the Star that reflects your Positioning that is unique, different, and better than all the competition in the marketplace, i.e., that is your reputation?

#2 Are you at least competitive on all of the four other points on the Star?

Value-Added Positioning

VALUE-ADDED STAR POSITIONING

YOUR COMPETITIVE BUSINESS ADVANTAGE – CREATING CUSTOMER VALUE THROUGH:

C = Personal Choice
Fashion, Control, Self, Customized, Tailored, Variety, Individuality, My/Me, Comprehensive Choices, Mass Customization

S = Caring Service
Personal Service, Values, Feeling Important, Customer Relationships, Respect, Caring, Feelings Emotions, Recovery Strategy, Integrity, Empathy, Sensitivity, Familiar, Trust, Cultural, Experience

Q = High Quality (Products & Services)
Features, Authentic, Simplicity, Information, Technology, Accuracy, Knowledge, Performance, Reliability, Functional, Durability, Uses, Consistency, Stability, Soundness, Unique, Innovative, Experiences

R = Delivery Responsiveness
Fast Delivery, Convenience, Methods, Timing, Speed, Distribution, Flexibility, Access, Ease of Doing Business, Support Services, Delivery Channels, Cooperation

T = Total Cost
Psychological Cost, Price, Life Cycle, Risk, Opportunity Costs, Waste/Environment, Working Conditions, Product/Services Costs

Service

Customer

CREATING CUSTOMER VALUE

Value Proposition:

Brand/Recognition/Positioning = Perceived Customer Value = $\dfrac{\text{Outputs}}{\text{Inputs}}$ = $\dfrac{\text{What I Get}}{\text{What I Must Give}}$ = Benefits

Mission Development Triangle Exercise

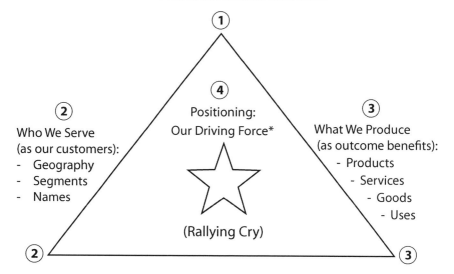

① Why We Exist
(If not already in vision statement)
- Societal Need
- Stockholder/Stakeholder Need

④
Positioning:
Our Driving Force*

(Rallying Cry)

②
Who We Serve
(as our customers):
- Geography
- Segments
- Names

③
What We Produce
(as outcome benefits):
- Products
- Services
- Goods
- Uses

Not in Your Mission:

How We Operate

- Values, Beliefs, Philosophies
- Major Activities, Techniques, Support Services
- Technologies, Methods of Sales/Distribution, Capacity
- Core Strategies
- Core Competencies and Capabilities

---

*Note: Your Driving Force/Positioning can be either a who, a what, a why, (1-2-3), but it must position you in the marketplace differently from your competitors.

Organizational Values Exercise
("Guides to Behavior")

Complete Column #1 (The Way It Should Be). Select 10 of the following values that have the most importance to your organization's future success.

Complete Column #2 (The Way It Is Now).

Column #1 The way it should be	Column #2 The way it is now	
_____	_____	1. Adaptation to Change
_____	_____	2. Long Term Strategic Perspective/Direction
_____	_____	3. Energizing/Visionary Leadership
_____	_____	4. Risk Taking
_____	_____	5. Innovation/Creativity
_____	_____	6. Marketplace Aggressiveness/Competitiveness
_____	_____	7. Teamwork/Collaboration
_____	_____	8. Individual/Team/Organization Learning
_____	_____	9. Recognition of Achievements
_____	_____	10. Waste Elimination/Wise Use of Resources
_____	_____	11. Profitability/Cost Conscious
_____	_____	12. Quality Products/Services
_____	_____	13. Customer Service Excellence/Focus
_____	_____	14. Speed/Responsiveness
_____	_____	15. Continuous/Process Improvement
_____	_____	16. Growth/Size of Organization/Revenue
_____	_____	17. Contribution to Society/Community
_____	_____	18. Safety
_____	_____	19. Stability/Security
_____	_____	20. Ethical and Legal Behavior
_____	_____	21. High Staff Productivity/Performance

Column #1 The way it should be	Column #2 The way it is now	
_____	_____	22. Employee Development/Growth/Self-Mastery
_____	_____	23. Dialogue/Openness and Trust
_____	_____	24. Constructive Confrontation/Problem Solving
_____	_____	25. Respect/Caring for Individuals/Relationships
_____	_____	26. Quality of Work Life/Morale
_____	_____	27. High Staff Satisfaction
_____	_____	28. Employee Self-Initiative/Empowerment
_____	_____	29. Participative Management/Decision-Making
_____	_____	30. Data-Based Decisions
_____	_____	31. Diversity and Equality of Opportunity
_____	_____	32. Partnerships/Alliances
_____	_____	33. Excellence in All We Do

CHAPTER 6
Phase B: Key Success Measures

Phase B: Quantifiable Outcome Measurements of Success
(The Feedback Loop)

"Goal setting and careful goal selection are the #1 criteria for success."

The second phase of this model consists of one significant step:

STEP #3: Key Success Measures (KSM)

In this step you develop the quantifiable outcome measurements (or Goals) of success in achieving an organization's vision, mission, and core values on a year-by-year basis. This is necessary to ensure continual improvement toward achieving the Ideal Future Vision. Key Success Measures/Goals enable concrete answer to three critical questions:

1. How do you know if you are being successful?

2. How do you know if you are getting into trouble?

3. If off course, what corrective actions should you take?

Key Success Measures (KSMs or Goals) should always measure what is really important (not just what is easy to measure) including, as a minimum,

1) customer satisfaction

2) employee satisfaction

3) financial viability

4) key operational indicators

5) community/societal contributions.

Typical other measures include product quality, customer service, internal zero defects vs. standards, cost vs. value, speed, delivery, response time, choice and customization, as well as being environmentally responsive.

Once KSM Areas are defined, specific measurements and yearly targets for each KSM Area are set. Ten is the maximum preferred number of KSMs, forcing a focus on what is really "key" to success. Use a "Key Success Measures Continuous Improvement Matrix" like the chart on the next page to plot, track, and report on your success.

Example: Canadian Standards Corporation had KSMs for service value, service quality, employee satisfaction, and financial viability. As an integrated information services firm serving the public sector, these KSMs were crucial to achieve their Vision. Financial viability alone is necessary to that vision, but is insufficient to fulfill it. Their failure to understand all their customers' needs led to their downfall.

Note: There is a popular approach (and book) called "The Balanced Scorecard." Their four measurement areas are similar to ours, just not (5) societal contributions. They came to the same conclusions that we did years before.

Key Success Measure Continuous Improvement Matrix (Backwards Thinking)

KSM Overall Coordinator for Accountability is _____ (Name / Title)

KSM Areas (Headers) with Specific Measures for Each	Baseline Target	Intermediate Targets		Target	Ultimate Target	Competitive Benchmark	KSM Accountability
	2006	2007	2008 2009	2010			
1. Header: Measures:							1.
2.							2.
3.							3.
4.							4.
5.							5.

NOTES:

CHAPTER 7
Phase C: Assessment to Strategies

Phase C: Converting Strategy to Operations (The Input to Act)

"If you don't know where you're going, any road will get you there."

This phase of the Three-Year Business Planning Model takes stock of current conditions and establishes core strategies as the organizing framework to guide the rest of the "Cascade of Planning" from the strategic to the operational to the individual levels.

STEP #4: Current State Assessment
(Ten Minimum Assessment Areas)

In traditional forms of Business Planning, this is the first and main step, leading to a long-range planning approach that merely projects the current state of an organization incrementally into the future. They do not use Destination Thinking first as progressive organizations in the 21st century do.

This step is where internal and external analyses (Strengths, Weaknesses, Opportunities, and Threats – SWOTs) are conducted. Then, the gaps between those analyses and the organization's vision are examined. Most organizations limit their analysis to SWOT, but this technique, by itself, is not enough.

The good news about the history of Business Planning is that there are numerous tools to use in conducting these analyses. We have developed a list of ten assessments each organization should do as a minimum (see page on this in this chapter).

Instructions: When conducting your Current State Assessment, it is important to conduct at least a minimum number amount of analysis and scanning. The following are recommended minimums. Please complete this task to ensure that these assessments are conducted as part of your Business Planning.

Note: The Current State Assessment, Step 4, is one place where Strategic Planning and Business Planning do differ. In Business Planning, this is where an organization actually competes with other organizations with their products and services and for their customer and market share. As a result, Business Planning should definitely include some "vital few" customer-market-products-services and competitor analysis.

What To Do	Who To Prepare It	By When
1. SWOT Analysis		
2. Business Excellence Architecture Best Practices		
3. SKEPTIC Environmental Scanning		
4. SBU/MPA Information		
– Pro Forma Matrix Today		
– Product/product line (market share and profitability)		
5. Organization financial analysis:		
– P/L (or budgets)		
– Balance sheet		
6. Core Values Analysis		
7. Key HR Processes		
8. "Focus on the Vital Few":		
– Positioning		
– Customer-Focused		
– Management/Leadership Skills		
9. Rewards for Total Performance		
10. All Key Success Measures (baseline data on KSM Matrix)		

Example: A Health System in California did a thorough analysis of each major health care system in their marketplace. These analyses were crucial in their deliberations on how to successfully compete in an industry of shrinking margins, tougher competition and calls for government to restructure and reform health care.

Specifically, this minimum list of ten assessment methods needed to include a systems way to assess an organization. To this end we developed an "Organization as a System" model (Business Excellence Architecture), built on the Baldrige Quality Award Criteria to address organizational assessment and fit to the overall Vision, Values, and Positioning.

The "Organization as a System" Model
(Business Excellence Architecture)

In trying to make the Systems Model come to life for organizational assessments and design in a more strategic specific and practical fashion, over 15 years ago we conducted a comprehensive literature search and identified over 13 Organization Models in use. However, when tested against the Systems Model, *all of them were found lacking; most because of a failure to focus on the customer and this Positioning need, mentioned earlier.*

Positioning to Create Customer Value is a simple three-step process that includes the Business Excellence Architecture.

Step #1 is a holistic, intensive focus on your customer's wants and needs for receiving value from you, now and in the future. *It must be the vision and driving force for your whole organization.* Using our Star Model to define this is the first step.

Step #2 is simple (right?) – implement the needed changes with a passion for "watertight integrity" to keep all the parts of the organization fitting together in support of your defined Positioning.

Step #3 consists of radically and strategically redesigning and re-aligning the entire spectrum of your business design, processes, and competencies to create this customer value. It also means redesigning the fundamental support and capacity-building components of your people and your collective leadership to better fit, integrate, and be attuned with this vision.

This third step is an organizational redesign so that all the parts and components of the organization fit and leverage each other. It is best depicted by our *"Business Excellence Architecture"* Hexagon Model beginning with Element #1, Performance Excellence.

Element #1: Building a Culture of Performance Excellence

The need to develop an organization's culture and core values for positioning the organization's uniqueness in the marketplace is crucial to achieving your performance excellence. Element #1 includes four key items:

1. A culture of innovation and creativity.
2. Language, thought processes, and practical tools of Systems Thinking.
3. Fact-based decision-making with good information and analysis.
4. A set of core values that create the desired culture.

Element #2: Reinventing Strategic Planning
(and the Key Here - Positioning)

Positioning for Value is in the eyes of the beholder. As previously stated, it is defined as "what the customer perceives that is unique, different and

ENTERPRISE-WIDE ASSESSMENT

through

THE BUSINESS EXCELLENCE ARCHITECTURE

THE SYSTEMS THINKING APPROACH™ TO CREATING YOUR COMPETITIVE BUSINESS ADVANTAGE

A — CREATING CUSTOMER VALUE #8

Choice · Service · Responsive · Cost · Quality

B — Quadruple Bottom Line™ Results
- Customers
- Employees
- Shareholders
- Society

E — FUTURE ENVIRONMENTAL SCAN

"STRATEGIC" BUSINESS **DESIGN**"

RESULTS

D

#2 REINVENTING STRATEGIC PLANNING

#3 LEADING ENTERPRISE-WIDE CHANGE

#7 ALIGNING DELIVERY AND DISTRIBUTION

#1 BUILDING A PERFORMANCE CULTURE

#4 CREATING THE PEOPLE EDGE

#6 BECOMING CUSTOMER FOCUSED

#5 ACHIEVING LEADERSHIP EXCELLENCE

"WATERTIGHT - AIRTIGHT INTEGRITY"

C — ENTERPRISE-WIDE ASSESSMENTS · BEST PRACTICES ·

© 2004 Stephen G. Haines, Centre for Strategic Management®
Website: www.csmintl.com · Phone: (619) 275-6528

EWA-BEA-Simple.eps

better when they choose to use your products and services in relationship to the 'total cost' (financial, psychological, environmental, and otherwise) of doing business with you instead of your competitor."

In systems terms, positioning is the "output" customers receive in return for giving their "inputs." It is the multiple outcomes they desire from the range of the five World Class Star ★ Results we found in our research.

In the 21st century, the competitive advantage will lie in positioning the organization overall to Create Customer Value, yet customizing it for each market segment and ultimately each individual customer.

Element #3: Leading Strategic Change

Overall management of cultural transformation to a customer-focused organization is crucial in this Element. This requires flexible, responsive people, participative norms of behavior, and empowered work settings. This change is led by setting up specific change management structures. They are the glue to keep all these change tasks on track and prevent status quo behaviors from prevailing.

This transformation involves people and social/emotional attunement through understanding and managing the process of change we call "The Rollercoaster of Change™."

This change is very difficult due to the defensive routines involved in letting go of the past and nurturing the persistence and resiliency required for a transformation between the old and new. Communication and rein-forcement plans are also essential to change individual behavior over time. Organizational change is a misnomer; organizations change only when people do – one by one.

During a transformation, teamwork is needed everywhere, including department and cross-functional teams, and on internal and external business processes. The key to success is horizontal cooperation and collaboration to serve the customer, not a vertical hierarchy/bureaucracy. These teams work far better if they are initially trained in Systems Thinking and Innovation. In fact, "Innovation Teams" is the right term!

Element #4: Creating the People Edge™

A key approach to customer value is having the "soft" people and support elements strategically "in tune" to achieve ongoing World Class Star ★ Results.

Strategic People/HR Management practices and the system of people management must be attuned to create "The People Edge." These practices include attracting, hiring, motivating, developing, empowering, rewarding, and retaining all crucial staff. (Our HRM Systems model and diagnostics detail this vital area. Call us for information or get our free article on it at www.csmintl.com.)

Element #5: Achieving Leadership Excellence

Leadership and management competencies, skills, and strategic communications practices are needed at all levels to ensure these "Star Results" are achieved. The management skills of trainer, coach, conflict-resolver, and facilitator are vital as are the abilities to become passionate customer advocates for and develop close relationships with the customer.

Leadership is the foundation for everything, and leadership development must be an initial and ongoing priority for the collective management team. This is especially true for the middle and senior executives of the organization who need all six levels of our natural leadership competencies, which are:

I.   Enhancing Self-Mastery

II.   Building Interpersonal Relationships

III. Facilitating Empowered Teams

IV.   Collaborating Across Functions

V.   Integrating Organizational Outcomes

VI. Developing Strategic Positioning

Element #6: Becoming Customer-Focused

Becoming customer-focused includes:
- Strategic marketing, sales planning, and implementation
- Choices and customization controlled by the customer
- Quality products and services delivered through TQM concepts (Deming, Juran, Crosby, etc.)
- High quality customer service (legendary, raving fans, etc.)
- The total cost of doing business with you is what it costs the customer – keep it low

In addition, the need for strategic budgeting and resource allocation to support all the selected priorities is crucial. It takes resources of all types, including people, money, facilities, space, technology, and information, etc., to make customer value a basic instinct throughout the entire firm.

Element #7: Aligning Delivery and Distribution

The last key to success in Creating Customer Value is to strategically realign the entire delivery system to provide this value to the customer every time. The Model highlights the many organizational elements that require strategic realignment toward your desired customer vision of World Class Star ★ Results.

These "Star Results" must be delivered through operational, value-added Supply Chain Management (supplier - employee -customer) including:

- Process improvement - including the "continuous improvement" (or Kaizen) concept
- Enterprise-wide technology, organizational design, restructuring, and technology tools are necessary to make sure all of the organization is supportive in Creating Customer Value
- Increased simplicity and reduction of waste and bureaucracy
- On time delivery, convenience, speed, and customer responsiveness

Summary on Organizational Culture
and the Organization as a System Model

The seven elements of our Business Excellence Architecture need to fit, align, attune, and integrate with each other in support of the customer. *Remember, the essence of the "Organization as a System" is not these elements alone, but rather their "fit and synergy together" in one synergistic "design," supporting the whole organization's Vision and customers' needs.*

The "whole" is what we often call an organization's "Culture." The issue of fit, alignment, and attunement helps to explain why culture is so resistant to change. When we change one aspect of how an organization functions, the change often conflicts with and meets with resistance from the other elements that are not being changed. The key issue with this Systems Framework is the "fit", linkage, and relationships among the elements. It is NOT finding the "best answer or technique or process" for each element, department, or unit. That type of "best" approach sub-optimizes the whole. It is the synergy of each unit and element working together in a coordinated and related fashion that breeds excellence.

In other words: Excellence is a matter of doing 10,000 little things right across all elements of an *Organization as a System*. And, since everything everywhere now affects everything else, the key to success is a disciplined fit of the entire system working together in support of the customer.

Thus, to change your culture to a customer-focused organization means that, in some fashion, you have to change all the elements of the System.

No wonder you might ask, "When culture and strategy collide, which wins out? Why, culture, of course!"

This also explains why most of the management writings today focus on more than one aspect of changing an organization; however, this is still only a partial system's solution.

If you are serious about a real cultural and values change, you have to "attack" it directly. Mere gradual change that doesn't upset anyone will never get you there. The radical approach to cultural change requires:

1. Attack the change radically, directly, and continually with your senior management's leadership behavior, as well as rewards and recogni-

tion processes, both formally and informally.

2. Change all seven modules together to fit differently in support of the new culture. Be ruthless about this need for fit and synergy.

3. Assess and be strident about changing as many aspects of your organization as possible to fit these new values (see the following Core Values Assessment and Uses).

In any case, these seven modules in the Business Excellence Architecture represent all the parts, or building blocks of an organization when viewed in system's terms. In addition, there is one more essential element of an "Organization as a System" that is needed to be assessed in order to change it to a "Customer-Focused" organization: the change process itself.

The Change Process acts as a "governor" for all the other elements. In order to change an organization and become customer-focused, you must "be a maniac with a mission" to pay attention to the change process and manage it strategically. Otherwise, all the desired changes and good intentions will lose out to these daily crises.

Core Values Assessment And Uses

The following are typical categories in which Core Values should appear and be reinforced in an organization. Where else should they appear and be reinforced?

1. Strategy
   - Explicit corporate philosophy/value statement – display as visuals
2. Operational Tasks
   - Corporate and product advertising
   - New customers and suppliers vs. current customer and supplier treatment and focus
   - Operational tasks of quality and service
3. Leadership
   - Flow of orientation and assimilation
   - Job aids/descriptions
   - To whom and how promotions occur, criteria
   - New executive start-up
   - Executive leadership ("walk the talk"), ethical decisions, how we

     manage

4. Resources/Technology/Communications
   - Internal communication (vehicles/pubs)
   - Press releases, external publications
   - Image nationwide
   - Resource allocation decisions
5. Structure
   - Dealing with difficult times/issues (i.e., layoffs, reorganizations)
   - Organization and job design questions
6. Processes
   - Recruiting handbook, selection criteria
   - How applicants are treated vs. values
   - How "rewards for performance" operates, especially non-financial rewards
   - Role of training, training programs
   - Performance evaluation, appraisal forms (assess values adherence), team rewards
   - Policies and procedures (HR, finance, administrative, etc.), day-to-day decisions
7. Teams
   - Cross-departmental events, flows, task forces
8. Macro
   - Managing change according to values
   - Stakeholder relationships vs. values
9. Feedback
   - This analysis
   - Employee survey

Quick Core Values Assessment and Why?

Best 2-3	1-2 Most in Need of Improvement
1.	1.
2.	
	2.
3.	

- 360° Feedback

The Importance of a Strategic Change Leadership Team

In every case where we have installed a Strategic Change Leadership Team to guide a large scale change project or to implement a business plan we have developed, implementation was quite successful. In the three cases where the organization's leadership did NOT install this Strategic Change Leadership Team, their implementation floundered. This Change Leadership Team is absolutely essential to track, monitor, report, and correct the planned changes so they have the desired result. In customer-focused, high performing organizations, strategic change is proactive and system-wide across all these seven modules of the Business Excellence Architecture, just phased in over time, based on priorities. In more traditional organizations, change is dealt with as isolated incidents and projects. In reactive organizations change is at an "avoid pain only" level, with very little follow-through.

Example: The City of Saskatoon is a wonderfully unknown Canadian city of 200,000 people with a beautiful River Valley running along the downtown edge. Once they completed their Strategic and Business Plans for all of their departments, they set up a Corporate Change Leadership Team which meets monthly to ensure that the desired changes actually take place.

Example: At the Washington Suburban Sanitation Commission, in the D.C. Region, senior executives and the top fifteen managers meet every month to discuss Strategic Change Management to ensure that their changes do not take three years, as predicted. They said they couldn't wait that long!

Note: Keep in mind:
> A paradigm shift in one aspect of an organization
> (i.e., mission – strategy – vision – culture)
> causes the need for paradigm shifts
> in every aspect of that organization
> (i.e., staffing – structure – technology – leadership, etc.)
> – if –
> you believe in systems view of Organizations.

Once your organizational assessment and SWOT is complete, now you are ready for Strategy Development, Step #5.

CHAPTER 8
Phase C-D: Strategy Development

STEP #5: Strategy Development

"If you always do what you've always done,
you'll always get what you've always gotten."

Step #5 creates the core strategies to bridge the gaps between the Ideal Future Vision (Phase A) and the Current State Assessment (Phase C). It results in the development of three to seven core strategies to be implemented unit-wide. These strategies become the organizing principles and priorities used by everyone as a design framework to set annual department and individual goals.

Each core strategy usually needs a set of 5 to 15 strategic action items to achieve that strategy over the three-year planning horizon. These strategic action items are the major activities, organizational priorities, and changes required over time that help achieve the Three-Year Business Unit Plan.

Further, you need to identify the top three action priorities for each strategy over the next 12 months. These provide direction for everyone in setting their annual, department, and individual goals for the next year. We call them the "must do" action priorities for the organization or business unit as a whole.

The 1990s saw a proliferation of new strategies as businesses tried to cope with revolutionary times. They included:

- Flexibility and opportunistic in looking for bargains (Giant Industries of AZ, as mentioned later)
- Business Process Re-engineering/Six Sigma (General Electric and others)
- Speed of product development (Toyota and Chrysler)
- Horizontal Integration of related products and by-products (AM/PM Mini Marts). Also, Ethanol Plants in Saskatchewan tie in grain farming, mash for cattle, steam generation and transportation
- Networks and Alliances (Apple/Microsoft or Japanese Kieretsu's)
- Value-Added consumer bargains (larger package at the same price

or Nissan selling their Maxima as a "Luxury Sedan")
- Environmentally Improved or Based Products such as solar heat, re-cycling, and toxic waste clean up
- Mass Customization (Toyota can deliver the exact car you want, with all its features in just two weeks) in Japan
- Rollups of small companies to create dominance (BFI-waste-management)
- Experiences (Rainforest and Hard Rock Cafes)
- Value Chain Management through teamwork among customers – manufacturers and suppliers

Now, in the 21st Century, with a Global Economy, what new strategies do you need for your business Unit, Program, or Function?

Are they the strategies of Speed, Outsourcing, New Technology, Experiences, Service, Alliances, Globalization, or Lower Costs?

In the public sector there is a similar set of strategies now being implemented.

13 Strategies of Entrepreneurial Government

1. Steer, not row (facilitate vs. do it yourself)
2. Empower communities and customers to solve their own problems rather than simply deliver services
3. Encourage competition rather than monopolies
4. Be driven by missions, not rules
5. Be results-oriented by funding outcomes rather than inputs
6. Meet the needs of the customer, not the bureaucracy
7. Concentrate on earning and making money rather than spending it
8. Stop subsidizing everyone. "User-pay" through charging user fees
9. Invest in preventing problems rather than curing crises
10. Decentralize authority
11. Solve problems by influencing market forces rather than creating public programs
12. Reduce regulations; cut out bureaucracy and low risk taking

13. Privatization (except for essentials not provided elsewhere)

In looking at your strategies, beware of those that are usually of the "Cost Cutting" variety only. These might include reorganizations, layoffs, business re-engineering, budget cutbacks, etc. "Cutting" is definitely necessary yet not sufficient for success. "Building" for the future type strategies focused on quality products and services that satisfy the customer is where the right answers are found. "Cutting and Building" strategies are absolutely BOTH needed!

We have found it extremely helpful to define how strategies are changing. A "From   To" simple set of phrases, like the sample below makes

---

Example: CORE STRATEGIES (From To)

1. Make TQM happen
   From: *Buzzword*   **To:** *Culture*

2. Create a customer focused organization
   From: *Inward focus*   **To:** *Customer focus*

3. Modernize Management Information System
   From: *Piecemeal*   **To:** *Systems Solution*

4. Manage the implementation and execution of the Business Plan
   From: *Business Planning*   **To:** *Change Management*

5. Enhance our development and effectiveness as members of the PWC team
   From: *People as cost*   **To:** *People as assets*

---

it crystal clear what the desired future state is to be.

STEP #6: Annual Organization-Wide Priorities

Once your Core Strategies and the "From - To" phrases are clear, now is time to develop the 10-15 or more action items necessary to achieve this strategy over the life of the Business Plan. Develop these, then identify the top three action priorities to achieve in the next 12 months for each of your Core Strategies.

These Core Strategies and Yearly Action Priorities become the "glue" and organizing framework for annual plans and strategic budgets. They force the Business Unit, Program, or Function to think, plan and act strategically and systems-wise in terms of shared strategies, not departments and turf battles. Now everyone is working towards the same ends in the next year (the "must do" action priorities and their Core Strategies).

In order to ensure that everyone works together, we highly recommend you form Strategy Project Teams for each Core Strategy comprised of three to six senior/mid-level executives. These members need to volunteer and have a passion for each strategy so they become "Change Agents" with a passion to sponsor or champion each Core Strategy. They will also need a team leader who must be one of the senior executives of the organization in order to show the importance of each strategy. There must be a deliberate "plan-to-implement" and "project management process" to get the strategies off the ground and moving.

In this fashion, you are developing as many as 42 leadership advocates for the future (seven strategies times 6 change agents each) to counteract the pull and resistance of today's organization and the status quo. Without Strategy Project Teams, the future is an orphan and will lose out to the day-day.

TURNAROUNDS, RENEWALS, AND BUSINESS PLANNING
(Selecting Your Strategies)

Follow the Rollercoaster of Change™ Sequence

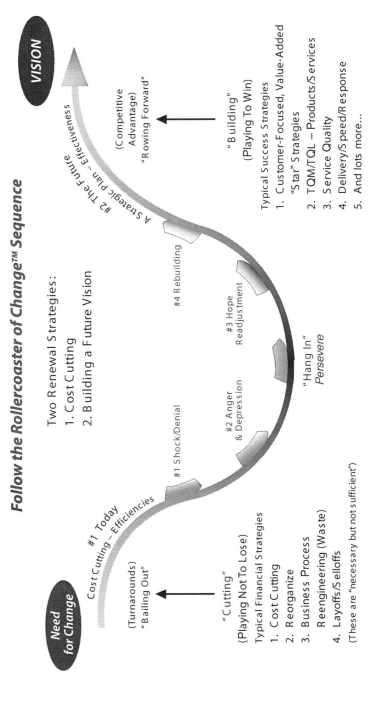

Two Renewal Strategies:

1. Cost Cutting
2. Building a Future Vision

VISION

Need for Change

#2 The Future – Effectiveness

A Strategic Plan

(Competitive Advantage)
"Rowing Forward"

"Building"
(Playing To Win)

Typical Success Strategies

1. Customer-Focused, Value-Added "Star" Strategies
2. TQM/TQL – Products/Services
3. Service Quality
4. Delivery/Speed/Response
5. And lots more...

#4 Rebuilding

#3 Hope
Readjustment

"Hang In"
Persevere

#2 Anger
& Depression

#1 Shock/Denial

Cost Cutting – Efficiencies

#1 Today

(Turnarounds)
"Bailing Out"

"Cutting"
(Playing Not To Lose)

Typical Financial Strategies

1. Cost Cutting
2. Reorganize
3. Business Process Reengineering (Waste)
4. Layoffs/Selloffs

(These are "necessary but not sufficient")

NOTES:

CHAPTER 9
Phase C-D: Annual Plans

STEP #7: Annual Plans and Strategic Budgets

"Excellence is a matter of doing 10,000 things right."

Step #7 is where "the rubber meets the road." It is where you develop Department plans with prioritized tasks and then allocate the resources to actually implement your core strategies and next 12 months action priorities.

As mentioned, each department needs a 12-month annual department plan using the same format with the Core Strategies as the organizing framework or "department goals." That format is on the next page. Using the top three priorities under each core strategy focuses the entire organization.

It is not enough for department's to develop their own isolated annual department plans, even if they have the same Core Strategies as each Department's Goals. These plans must be coherent as an organization, and suppport each other department. To do this, a yearly Large Group Review Meeting of the full collective leadership (i.e., top 30-50 people) where all department plans are critiqued and refined, based on their fit with the strategies and yearly top organization-wide priorities.

To truly become strategic, it is often necessary to also change the way budgeting is traditionally done. Budgeting needs to be more strategic and follow (not lead) annual planning. This will enable you to achieve a more focused allocation of resources based on the strategic plan and your top three priority "must do's" actions under each core strategy.

The tension between current allocations vs. future priorities is normal and desired. In many cases, internal "Request For Proposal" (RFP) systems are set up to promote short-term projects that move the vision forward. A listing of 10 new ways to do "Strategic Budgeting" may also help a very difficult budget process:

Ten Ways to Establish Your Budget and Resource Allocation Approach

Approach #1: Macro allocations only (let managers decide "how to")

Approach #2: Activity level budgeting (zero-based)

Approach #3: Require 5-10-15% budget cut projections and plans (cut different amounts though)

Approach #4: Budget "hold-backs" (create a pool of funds) for strategic priority uses

Approach #5: Recommend New Initiative Programs (NIPS) for all funding increases

Note: The next five approaches are too late to begin at strategic budgeting time. You need to start them earlier in the year, so that their results in cost savings will be evident at budgeting time.

Approach #6: "Workout" the bureaucracy and eliminate "waste"

Approach #7: Reengineer your business' economic structure and process

Approach #8: Learning as a critical resource and increased skills and motivation

Approach #9: Recognition and rewards programs

Approach #10: Fund raising

Cascade of Planning Key

Lastly, we Cascade the Planning down to the individual accountability level. Once the Annual Plan and Budget is in place, at least three other crucial management systems must be installed if you are serious about Business Planning and Superior Results:

#1 Performance Management System

#2 Rewards and Recognition System

#3 Performance Appraisals - tied to support:
- Your Core Strategies (i.e. results) and
- Your Core Values (i.e. behaviors)
- Each person's learning / development needs (i.e., career development)

"What we think, or what we know, or what we believe is, in the end,

Annual Work Plan Format
(For Functional/Division/Department Plans)

Date: _____

Fiscal Year: _____

Strategies/Goals: (What) _____

Yearly Pri#	Strategic Action Items (Actions/Objectives/How?)	Support/Resources Needed	Who Responsible?	Who Else to Involve?	When Done?	Optional How to Measure?	Status

NOTES:

CHAPTER 10
Phase D: Implementation

of little consequence. The only thing that matters ... is what we do. "

STEP #8: Plan-To-Implement

Step #8 is the bridge between Business Planning and strategic change; bridging from Goal #1 (Planning) to Goal #2 (Implementation).

This Plan-to-Implement step is generally completed at a one-day offsite much as the Plan-to-Plan Step #1.

Plan-to-Implement: A.M.

The morning is an "Educational Briefing" about Strategic Change. It is organized around the "Iceberg Theory of Change" (see next page). First we cover "why change efforts fail" (see following pages). It might be useful to take this exercise now and see where your strengths and weaknesses are in managing change.

Why Change Efforts Usually Fail

"Most companies don't fail for lack of talent or strategic vision.
They fail for lack of execution – the routine 'blocking and tackling'
that great companies consistently do well and always strive to do better."

- T. J. Rodgers, No-Excuses Management

To understand what you do or are likely to fail to do at implementation, circle the following #s that apply:

1. Underestimate Systems Complexity. Top level executives tend to underestimate what it will take. They have unrealistic expectations and fail to understand that the organization is a system of interdependent parts and different levels (individual, team, organization). Thus, knee-jerk simple and direct cause and effect solutions dealing with symptoms only, is the result.

2. Details Lacking. The failure to specify in sufficient detail the actual work required to implement the change at all levels of the organization.

3. **Change Knowledge Missing.** The failure to know, follow and use the "Rollercoaster of Change" as to how people go through change

THE ICEBERG THEORY OF CHANGE
The Systems Thinking Approach™

(The CAPACITY* to Achieve Your Competitive Business Advantage)

Efforts:

13%

What's Your...

87%

1. CONTENT
What
(Visible)

"Alignment" – Operational Tasks
(Customer Edge)
- Customer ★ Results
- Delivery Processes

... Level of Capacity*

2. PROCESSES – How
(Below the Surface)

"Attunement" – wth People's
Hearts (People Edge)
- Support Content
- Rollercoaster Uses
- Change Processes

COMPETENCIES
RESOURCES

＊3. STRUCTURES – Framework
(Deep Foundation)

"Systems Thinking"
(Strategic Edge)
- Change Structures
- Organizational
  Capabilities
- Culture

＊CULTURE/COMMITMENT

CONTENT MYOPIA

is our failure to focus on Process and Structure.

Yet,

Change is dependent on good Processes and Structures

in order to Achieve the Content of the desired changes.

psychologically. That change has three dimensions – cultural, political, and rational. Discounting the cost of the psychological effects of change or not sufficiently investing in human assets.

4. **Reinforcers Lacking.** The lack of realignment of the business control systems such as performance measures, budgets, IT, compensation, values. Absence of support and reinforcement/rewards for the new changes.

5. **Accountability Failure.** The lack of specific accountability, responsibility and consequences at every level of the organization. Inadequate executive accountability and leadership of the change – failure to know their role is the active "champions" of the changes.

6. **Time Pressure.** Too many changes at once and a quick-fix mentality. Too short-term an orientation by the senior executives. Even greed, obsession with short-term, fast buck, and super profits. Failure to budget adequate "lead" or "lag" time.

7. **Management Resistance.** Middle and first line management resistance, apathy, or abdication.

8. **Turf Battles.** Opposing or conflicting messages, turf battles among departments or instigated by top management, and split views among executives act as cancers upon the change efforts. A lack of focused, clear direction, or poor teamwork, and conflict is the usual result.

9. **Change Structures Missing.** Lacking the formal structures, processes, and required dedicated resources to lead and follow-up on the desired changes.

10. **Reactive Posture.** The failure to act in a proactive fashion; allowing issues to fester and grow, or reacting in a eclectic fashion without a plan or organized framework and philosophy.

11. **Status Quo.** Vested interests and power in the status quo, an auto-pilot mindset or complacency within the hierarchy can defeat most change efforts. Habits are hard to break.

12. **Stubbornness.** Stupidity and stubbornness by senior management in not using proven research on what works. Instead, relying on their own inadequate models of change, mindless imitation of the latest fad, or using outmoded theories of motivation.

13. **Control Issues.** Senior executive desire to maintain control over

people and events vs. strategic consistency and operational flexibility. Low tolerance for uncertainty and ambiguity condemns change to failure.

14. **Participative Management Skills Lacking.** Inadequate senior management knowledge and skills on what to do and how to manage change; Poor execution – the routine blocking and tackling that great organizations do consistently well. Lack of skills by managers and executives in "participative management" techniques; including those of trainer, coach, and facilitator. The organization chart is designed to run the day- to-day as efficiently as possible, and to resist change and variation.

15. **Fatal Assumption.** Making the fatal assumption that "everyone is for change, understands it, and that execution is only a matter of following your natural inclinations.

16. **Redistribution Failure.** Failure to redistribute financial resources based on future priorities/direction through lack of strategic budgeting. Denial and unwillingness to make the required "tough decisions."

17. **Politically Correct Desire.** The perception that it isn't politically correct to be a strong leader with convictions, expertise, and strong directions/opinions. Putting up with poor performance.

18. **Initial Bias Wrong.** A bias towards thinking that initially communicating direction, educating people, forming teams, and holding meetings will result in success.

19. **Lack of Senior Management Modeling.** The unwillingness of senior management to model the desired changes first, thus, gaining credibility and trust towards the desired changes; Unwillingness to change their leadership and management practices/communications.

20. **Multiple Consultants and Philosophies.** Ineffective use of multiple consultants and/or philosophies on a piecemeal basis. Paradigms and belief in analytic approaches to a systems problem.

21. **Lack of Customer-Focus.** Failure to focus on customer wants, needs, and satisfaction as the main reason for existence.

22. **Skeptics Not Involved.** Failure to value skeptics and to enroll a critical mass for change. The lack of use of high involvement methods, the Parallel Involvement Process, and opportunities for personal and group growth and development.

23. **Poor Cross-Functional Teamwork.** Lack of horizontal, cross-functional communications, teamwork and collaboration.

24. **Unsupportive Organizational Design.** The organizational structure and design does not support the desired changes; there is no one coordinating the change on a day-to-day basis.

25. **Lack of Follow-Through.** The failure to follow-through and sustain the energy, momentum, buy-in and stay-in, effort and commitment. Lack of accountability and persistence over the long-term.

26. **Middle Manager Skills Lacking.** Failure to direct, train, empower, leverage, support, and build the skills of middle managers and first line supervisors.

27. **Poor Communication of Direction.** Poor communications and lack of clarity in stump speeches about the direction.

28. **Cherished Values Violated.** Violation of cherished values without clear understanding of why, and what replaces it.

29. **Failure to Debrief and Learn.** Failure to conduct postmortems, debriefs and distillation of learnings from previous change efforts.

30. **Lack of Cultural Awareness.** Failure to understand local, global, cultural or ethnic diversity – thus taking wrong, insensitive actions.

31. **Lack of a Game Plan.** Failure to have an "Implementation Game Plan" for the process of change.

32. **Political Environment.** The presence of a political and politicized environment and multiple agendas that block real progress.

33. **Powerlessness.** Inability to make decisions and change in a timely manner (paralysis/bottlenecking).

Why Change Efforts Usually Fail - Summary

1. Which 3-5 efforts are our change strengths? Why?

Strengths?	Why?
1.	
2.	
3.	
4.	
5.	

2. Which 3-5 mistakes do we usually make?

Mistakes?	Why?	Implications
1.		
2.		
3.		
4.		
5.		
6.		
7.		
8.		

A Menu of Required Change Structures

We next cover the deepest part of an iceberg - way below the surface of the water - the menu of "structures" needed to manage change effectively. Usually structures are ignored and not set in place - thus causing change efforts to fail before they ever get started. Remember it was the mass of ice beneath the surface that sunk the Titanic.

However, the Primary Change Management Structures are keys to beginning change with a high potential of success.

Primary Strategic Change Management: A Menu
(Structures and Roles)
Main Teams

1. Visionary Leadership – CEO/Senior Executives with Personal Leadership Plans
    - For repetitive stump speeches and reinforcement
    - To ensure fit/integration of all parts & people towards the same vision/values

2. Internal Support Cadre (informal/kitchen cabinet)
    - For day-to-day coordination of implementation process
    - To ensure the change structures & processes don't lose out to day-to-day

3. Executive Committee
    - For weekly meetings, follow up, and attention
    - To ensure follow-up on the top 15-25 priority yearly actions from the Strategic Plan

4. Strategic Change Leadership Team (CLT)
    - For formal monthly follow-up meetings to track, adjust and refine everything
    - To ensure follow-through via a yearly comprehensive map of implementation

Subcommittees of #4 Above:

*5. Strategy Project Teams
    - For each core strategy and major change effort
    - To ensure achievement of each strategy, including leadership of what needs to change

*6. Employee Development Board (Attunement With People's Hearts)
- For succession, careers, development, core competencies at all levels, and performance management/appraisals
- To ensure fit with our desired values and culture, and manage employees as a competitive edge

*7. Technology Steering Committee
- For computer, telecommunications, software fit and integration
- To ensure "system-wide" fit and coordination around information management

*8. Strategic Communications System and Structures
- For clear two way dialogue and understanding of the Plan and implementation
- To ensure everyone is heading in the same direction with the same strategies and values

*9. Measurement and Benchmarking Team
- For collecting and reporting of Key Success Measures, especially customers, employees and competitors
- To ensure an outcome and customer-focus at all times

10. Annual Department Plans
- For clear and focused department plans that are critiqued, shared and reviewed
- To ensure a fit, coordination and commitment to the core strategies and annual top priorities

11. Whole System Participation
- For input and involvement of all key stakeholders before a decision is made that affects them. Includes Parallel Involvement Processes, Search Conferences, and management conferences.
- To ensure a critical mass in support of the vision and desired changes

Subcommittees of #4: the Leadership Team

Change Processes:

Just below the surface of an iceberg, ever persistent but also rarely discussed, is the "process" of organizational change. We call it the Rollercoaster of Change™.

The Rollercoaster of Change™ Explained

It is a myth that there is such a thing as "Organizational Change." Change is an individual and psychological matter for each of us; the bigger the organization the more difficult it is to get everyone to change and focus on the customer. "The Rollercoaster of Change™" is a term Steve Haines coined a number of years ago for a phenomenon that naturally occurs and is written about in numerous fields and disciplines, especially mental health. While the terminology may be different, the dynamics are the same and the Rollercoaster is a reality of life. See it on the next page.

Example: The question is not "if" each employee will go through the Rollercoaster but when, how deep, how long will it take, and will they successfully reach the other side? This last question of reaching the other side successfully is quite an issue for most organizations. Many executives were trained in the skill of "telling" others what to do. In Rollercoaster of Change™ terms, "telling" is the "skill" of inducing shock and depression in your employees. It is a "given" that each of us will go through stages #2 and #3 of the Rollercoaster (shock and depression). However, going through stages #5 and #6 (hope and rebuilding) is optional and depends on someone leading and managing the change process effectively. The key is to know WIIFM (What's In It For Me) for each person.

How To Manage Large Scale Organizational Change

1. Clearly define and agree on the new Vision and Plan
2. Set up a "Change Management Leadership Team"
3. Manage the Rollercoaster of Change™
   a. How, where, and when to acknowledge the depression; explain the why face-to-face.
   b. How to build in hope, involvement, and WIIFM?

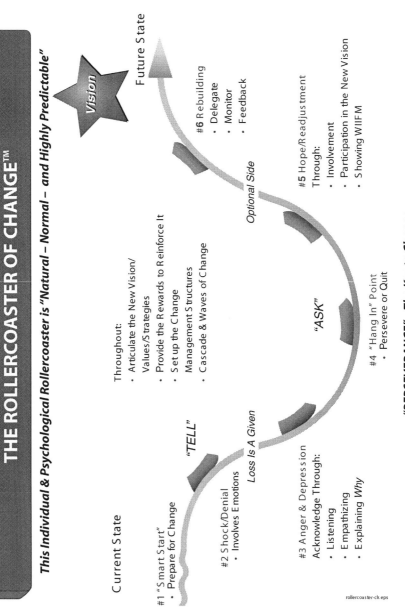

THE ROLLERCOASTER OF CHANGE™

This Individual & Psychological Rollercoaster is "Natural – Normal – and Highly Predictable"

Vision

Current State

Future State

#1 "Smart Start"
• Prepare for Change

"TELL"

Throughout:
• Articulate the New Vision/ Values/Strategies
• Provide the Rewards to Reinforce It
• Set up the Change Management Structures
• Cascade & Waves of Change

Loss Is A Given

#2 Shock/Denial
• Involves Emotions

#3 Anger & Depression
Acknowledge Through:
• Listening
• Empathizing
• Explaining *Why*

"ASK"

Optional Side

#4 "Hang In" Point
• Persevere or Quit

#5 Hope/Readjustment
Through:
• Involvement
• Participation in the New Vision
• Showing WIIFM

#6 Rebuilding
• Delegate
• Monitor
• Feedback

"PERSEVERANCE" – The Key to Change

rollercoaster-clr.eps

The other "Catch 22" of the Rollercoaster is that once you start through it, you cannot go back and erase what you began. Instead, attempting to reverse changes already in motion just kicks off another Rollercoaster; only this time from the spot at which you tried to reverse the process. Since this usually happens at Stage #3 (depression), it generally means that the new Rollercoaster will sink employees deeper down into depression. It rarely will get you out of the hole you are digging for yourself, your firm, and your employees. However, there are tools to help people through Stage #3 (depression)...listening, asking questions, empathizing, constantly explaining the Vision of the Future and letting people experience first-hand the executive's presence and rationale for the change.

However, the only way up the right hand (and optional) side of the Rollercoaster is through leadership and management. In other words, you must be Drucker's "monomaniac with a mission" to have "persistence, persistence, persistence" (Step #4) in implementing, correcting and improving the changes as you go. Both participation and involvement in the change are the key to rebuilding the hope of Stage #5.

In other words, depression is normal and to be expected as a resistance to change. The worst thing an executive can do is to "push" them further or tell them they "should not feel that way." The more resistance you feel and express to an employee by telling/pushing them, the more they will resist you as well (the action-reaction syndrome).

The Rollercoaster highlights just how difficult it is to create a critical mass in support of your desired changes. The importance of not only "Buy in" but getting people to "Stay-In" throughout the Rollercoaster and its bottoming out is critical. For an example of how this can go wrong, remember the former USSR, and Mikhail Gorbachev as he tried to reverse his 500-day market economy plan. Also remember the ex-communists of the old USSR's People's Congress as they tried to reverse Yeltsin's reform programs. The failure to reverse change was the end result of both – with chaos as a by-product.

In summation, the Rollercoaster of Change is natural, normal, and highly predictable. Ignore it at your own peril!

Plan-to-Implement Day: P.M.

The afternoon of this Plan-To-Implement Day is taken up with reviewing our Year #1 Strategic Change Process Checklist (see next page).

This is also a time to organize and establish a "Change Leadership Team" (CLT) to guide the changes spelled out by the Business Plan.

The CLT also develops a roll out and communications plan for the newly developed Business Planning Document. This document is finalized during this phase by using the KISS method (10-15 pages in desktop publishing format). This allows the Planning Document to be in a practical day-to-day fashion vs. the dreaded SPOT Syndrome (Strategic Plan On the Top Shelf) gathering dust.

Step #8 is also when the same 30-50 collective leaders participate in a three-day skill building workshop entitled "Leading Strategic Change." This workshop provides the knowledge and skills necessary to manage change successfully in more detail than this one-day Plan-To-Implement session.

Ultimately, a "Yearly Comprehensive Map" of all these implementation processes is developed to summarize your first year's game plan (see the following example). This becomes the final page in the Three-Year Business Planning Document.

The culmination of the afternoon is the presentation of "Personal Leadership Plans" by top management which highlight what they are personally committed to doing and leading to ensure Goal #2 (successful implementation.)

The afternoon is also when the Strategy Project Teams get involved and started as change agent teams who will track and report on each Core Strategy during Change Leadership Team meetings. The afternoon of the Plan-to-Implement day often allows them time to meet and get organized.

Example: A major California utility's marketing organization planned monthly Change Leadership Team meetings in order to "jump-start" their implementation in meeting rapidly changing customer demands. Achieving superior results faster was the welcomed outcome.

Summary - Plan-to-Implement Day
(Educate – Assess – Tailor – Organize)

I. Educate
1. Iceberg Theory of Change (content – process – structure)
2. Rollercoaster of Change
3. Menu of Structures for Change
4. 3 Goals, 3 Premises, ABCs Model
5. System of Innovation
6. Why Change Fails

II. Assess
1. Summary of Desired Major Changes (from the Strategic Plan)
2. Strategic Plan/Annual Plan completion
3. Year #1 Strategic Change Process
4. Leadership Development Assessment/System
5. Multi-year Cultural Change Effort (Executive Development)
6. "Business Excellence Architecture" ("Building on the Baldrige") Assessment
7. Innovation Audit

III. Tailor
1. Yearly Comprehensive Map of Implementation
2. Change Leadership Team
3. Performance/Rewards Form/System to Reinforce the Change
4. Rollout/Communicate to Organization
5. Strategic People Plan – "Creating the People Edge"
6. Implementing Transformational and Culture Change
7. "One Agenda – One Day" meetings on key nuggets
8. GoInnovate! System of Innovation

IV. Organize
1. Change Leadership Team
2. Project Management Office (PMO)
3. Project Teams
4. Internal/External Coordination (Change Agent Cadre)
5. Employee Development Board
6. Key Success Measure Tracking – measuring
7. Personal Leadership Plans

Strategic Change Leadership Team (CLT)

Phase I: Monthly as the process begins

Phase II: Bi-monthly once the process is functioning
            smoothly

Core Steering Group Roles

1. Steering Group is led by the top leader of the organization who coordinates regular weekly/monthly meetings of all the other members.

2. Internal Staff Overall Change Management Coordinator responsibility by a competent and credible senior level executive with the time/energy to coordinate the activities – supported by a competent assistant/ secretary support person.

3. Internal Communications Coordinator to ensure ongoing communications to all key stakeholders.

4. Key Success Measure Coordinator to ensure measures are tracked/reported regularly.

5. Internal Staff Facilitator involved and trained to take over some of the duties from the external consultant over time.

6. "Strategy Project Team Leaders" who are leaders of the cross-functional teams set up previously for each Core Strategy. If not set up, do so at this time.

7. Secretary and administrative support with a computer to take "minutes."

8. An external master consultant who is skilled in both this process and your content areas of change.

Change Leadership Team (Standard Meeting Agenda)

Note: These interactive Business Planning implementation follow-up days are designed to include learning, change management, and team building.

1. Welcome – Agenda – Logistics – Norms – "Last" To Do List Reviewed – Interactive "change" icebreaker.
   Where in the yearly planning cycle/map are we?

2. Review Status of Key Success Measures vs. targets (KSM Coordinator).

3. Learning Activity: Conduct communications and interpersonal skills, coaching, presenting, facilitating, team building or other change management skills needed to have the Committee work effectively.

4. Review Core Strategies, strategic change projects, and top priority annual action items (Strategic Sponsorship Teams/presenters – be interactive, questions and answers, etc.).

   • List top 3 successes to celebrate

   • List top 3 issues/concerns and problem solve them

   Note: Rollercoaster of Change – Each topic needs to answer three questions:

   a. Where are we as a team on this Rollercoaster?

   b. Where is the rest of the organization?

   c. What actions are needed to bring us through these desired changes?

5. Review of Annual Plan Status (or business/functional plans).

   • For each department, follow-up results obtained

   • Maintain the organization's "systems fit, alignment, and integrity" with any other major changes

6. Changing Priorities? Environmental Changes?

   • What are they? What to do about them?

7. Deepen Change Management Understanding and Assessment.

   Each meeting cover one new change management tool and apply it to an issue/strategy:

• Best Practices List	• High Performance Survey
• Wheel of Detail	• "Change Implications" List
• Empowerment Criteria	• Menu on Alignment and Attunement
• Cross-Functional Teams	• Leadership Development Competencies
• HR Management Practices	• Positioning and Customer Star Results

8. Communications to Key Stakeholders (Continue the Parallel Involvement Process)
   - In writing plus face-to-face
   - Stump speeches
   - Unit/department meetings also (cascade communications)
9. Next Steps
   - To Do List reviewed – assign accountability/timing
   - Next Change Leadership Team meeting – prepare agenda
   - Next year's timetable for our annual strategic review/planning and budgeting cycle?
10. Process – How did it go?
11. Who to involve (and How) is key in continuing a Parallel Involvement Process.

Who	How
1. Board of Directors	
2. Middle Managers	
3. All Employees	
4. External Stakeholders	

- Both the day and the Strategic Change Management process overall

Sample "Yearly Cycle" of the Strategic Management System

Date	**Task**
June – Year #1	1. Begin Business Planning (Plan-to-Plan: 1 day)
July – October	2. Do Business Planning (5-8 days overall)
November	3. Develop Annual Work Plans/Budgets *
January – Year #2	4. Conduct Large Group Dept. Plan Review (1 day) *
January	5. Conduct Plan-to-Implement (1 day) *
January - December	6. Monthly Change Leadership Team Review Session
July	7. A Semi-Annual Change Leadership Team Update Session
September	8. Evaluate Plan's Year #1 Success – Rewards based on this
October - December	9. Conduct Annual Strategic Review (& Update: 2-4 days overall) *
January – Year #3	10. Develop Updated Annual Department Work Plans/Budgets
January	11. Conduct Large Group Department Plan Review (1 day)
January - December	12. Monthly Change Leadership Team Review Session
October – December	13. Institutionalized – Strategic Review/Update Again – as a way of life

* These are the steps often missed – resulting in failure to successfully implement your Business Plan.

NOTES:

CHAPTER 11
Phase D: Strategy Implementation and Change

GOAL #2: Ensure Successful Implementation and Change
STEP #9: Strategy Implementation and Change

This step results in transforming the Business Plan into thousands of group and individual plans and efforts, and tying a rewards system to it. The integrity of all the organization parts fitting together in support of the Vision is very difficult to achieve and is a critical organization design issue. Human Resource issues and programs are one key. Your business processes are another. For instance, your performance appraisal should evaluate everyone on their behaviors vs. the Core Values and their contribution to results vs. the Core Strategies of the Business Plan.

Implicit in this step is the understanding that we have to manage change before it manages us (in ways we may not like). Monthly meetings of the Strategic Change Leadership Team are absolutely essential. No organization we have worked with has successfully implemented their Strategic Planning without an effective Change Leadership Team. Three agenda items are mandatory for each Change Leadership Team meeting:

1. Continually scanning the changing environment for Business Planning implications

2. Tracking, reporting and problem solving Key Success Measure issues

3. Reviewing status of core strategies and top priority actions

What Do We Mean By "Strategic Change"?
(And how do you actually accomplish it?)

Change is a word that is all around us today. It's often been said that "the only thing that's constant is change." Surprisingly, while one author was teaching at the Banff Centre for Management, not a single one of the 29 executives in the course had previously taken either a formal academic course on "Change" or an intensive skills training program on it!

Have you?

So, while change may be all around us, it does not necessarily mean we know how change occurs, or how to lead and manage it successfully. Many of us have "learned" about how to change something by having had it "done to us" earlier in our careers. So if we had autocratic bosses in the past, what we learned was probably the wrong way to do it.

Just what do we mean by "strategic change" and how does one manage it? First of all, strategic (or large scale) change must flow either from a strategic plan or from a strong thrust (or driving force) led by the CEO/Business Unit Head or Executive Director. Any time the business top executive is not focused on the change, chances are the change will be seen as a side program, and not essential to the business. This is what is happening with "Six Sigma" and "Balanced Scorecard" in a number of firms today. Initially, delegation (and ultimately abdication) by top management occurs; resulting in failure of the desired change.

Example: GM had a "Quality Network" set up jointly with the UAW, but only gave it lip service. As one author personally observed, the program was not seen as a Core Business Strategy, and was not working at GM or within most of its Business Units. GM, once the world's greatest corporation, is now breathing fumes, and does not have many miles left.

To synthesize the many tasks needed for systemic change into a useful listing, we have compiled the ten "Areas" to focus upon for effective Strategic Change.

So, if this is Strategic Change, how do I master it?

When looking at all of the issues with creating a customer-focused high performance organization, it should be obvious by now why change takes 3-5 years, even with concentrated and continual action. The issues in Mastering Strategic Change are many:

1. The need for a top executive of the business unit who is a persistent and focused leader.

2. The need for the Three-Year Business Plan and Core Strategies to guide the change.

3. The need to position the unit to navigate the dynamic and global mar-

ketplace.

4. The need to truly understand the customer's wants and needs better than our competition.

5. The need to understand and master the skills embedded in the Rollercoaster of Change™ (and all its nuances). Remember, it is natural, normal, and highly predictable.

6. The ability to create a critical mass in active support of the desired changes. Remember, "people support what they help create."

7. The need for the overall skills in leading and managing the changes so that they actually occur successfully, while still paying attention to day-to-day crises (i.e., a Leadership Development System).

8. Installing Strategic Human Resource Management practices to ensure people are part of your competitive edge.

9. A complete revamping of your "Organization Design" to fit with the core values and core strategies.

10. And lastly, the need to understand the concept and framework of an "Organization as a System" (Business Excellence Architecture) to ensure the "fit, alignment, attunement, and integrity" of all the elements.

Traditional, analytical or partial systems thinking will direct you to focus only on those organization elements of an that are important to you personally or professionally. However, the chances of you paying attention to ALL the needed elements or Modules of an organization are remote at best.

> *"If the best writers and management theorists of our time*
> *don't pay attention to all the elements, why do you think*
> *that you will pay attention to them all?"*

If the ten issues cited above are key to becoming a customer-focused high performance organization, then the question becomes, "at what level of Mastery am I now in my SKILLS of managing strategic change?"

In trying to answer that, consider that there are four potential skill levels of management professionalism:

#1 Trainee/Rookie or Journeyman (1st line supervisor),

#2 Technique-driven (management),

#3 Systems model or theory-driven/eclectic (middle management), and

#4 Mastery (or Jazz/strategic/Strategic) level (senior management).

It is commonly accepted that all disciplines or fields of endeavor have these four levels of professionalism. In the field of Strategic Change you may be similar to the Banff course executives noted earlier who lacked formal background in managing strategic change. This is especially true concerning executive skills in changing to or creating a customer-focused organization. This outcome of being customer-focus coupled with a quantifiable measurement system based on a Systems Thinking Framework is definitely NOT the norm for western business and society, or our management writers.

Our experience shows that most readers probably fall somewhere in the second skill level above when implementing change, "utilizing some comfortable techniques." But it's rare that those techniques are effective and result in the desired changes WITHOUT any unintended negative side effects in your organization or with your employees.

Unfortunately, the Change Mastery challenge facing most senior management is multifaceted:

#1 You must search out and eliminate your change techniques that produce unintended negative consequences

#2 You must master leading all the six steps in the Rollercoaster of Change™; not just the skill of telling (or inducing shock and depression)

#3 You have to learn how to use the "Organization as a System" framework in all that you do so it becomes second nature in how you think, act and lead

#4 You must also develop an "automatic pilot" mentality, as a companion to the above, that keeps EVERYTHING you and others do focused on the customer. Remember, the customer is the reason for your existence

#5   You will also need to develop the new skills of effective management and leadership: Trainer, Coach and Facilitator (again, your needed leadership development system).

Developing your thinking, managing and leading skills in the five areas above will raise your skills to the 3rd skill level of professionalism – the Systems Framework. This will result in a marked improvement in your ability to create a highly effective customer-focused organization. However, that still leaves the fourth level of Mastery to be attained by those who are responsible for, or desire to strategically and successfully lead, a large public or private organization of any type.

This fourth Level is being a true master in the practice of Strategic Change. This is analogous to being a professional "jazz" musician – able to perform in a freeform manner with virtuoso ability. You need that "jazz" ability in leading your organization – being able to think and act masterfully and strategically, under changing conditions, in the pursuit of satisfying (or exceeding) your customers' wants or your business units' needs successfully. This Mastery Level includes the ability to be flexible and authentic within your own personal style; dealing with the circumstances of the moment while holding true to your Vision, Strategies, and your customers' best interests. Yet, as a master, you are able to move "off the melody," so to speak, as a great jazz musician does, and still return to the Vision and Framework without missing a beat or straining your leadership credibility.

Example: The jazz musician-type leader welcomes making exceptions to policies, and reacts positively to innovations and creative ideas that normally make other executives uncomfortable. They also encourage trying any of the change menu elements that break with the status quo. Their primary question is how this creativity and innovation will improve the way they satisfy the customer. Flexibility, encouragement and positive reaction to employee creativity and innovations are what allows them the freedom to act, be empowered, take risks, and not be penalized for it. This is a key skill for today's executives to master; and it is what the Deming "Drive out Fear" principle was all about in his TQM system.

This senior management level mastery results in "Exceeding Customer Expectations," the only way to retain customer loyalty long term. Statistics have consistently shown that it is about 5 times as hard (and expensive) to find a new customer as it is to retain a current one.

Example: On a recent Friday, a travel agency forgot to deliver one of our associates' airplane tickets for a two week business trip, which was to begin the following day. Since he was traveling all across North America you can imagine the problems (and cost) this forgetfulness created. However, they handled it beautifully. Not only did he hear from the travel agent, but the agency owner went out of his way to call and try to help. They never denied the problem. Instead they sent him an apology card at his hotel in a foreign city. They also called to again apologize, sent champagne to his hotel room, and insisted on paying for any and all added costs he had incurred. They even gave us credits for future travel. This is what is meant by a "Recovery Strategy" and Unsurpassed Customer Service with your customers. Forget the policies and costs; just improvise, play jazz and exceed the customer's expectations in recovering from a mistake.

In summary, following-up and correcting mistakes (along with disciplined persistence and integrity) are key in Step #9.

In the next chapter, Step #10 includes an Annual Strategic Review and Update of the Business Plan – the key to sustaining your vision over the long term).

CHAPTER 12
Phase D: Annual Strategic Review and Update

"People do what we inspect. Not what we expect."

GOAL #3: Sustaining High Performance
STEP #10: Annual Strategic Review and Update

This step is similar to a yearly independent financial audit and includes:

1) Reacting to changes in the environment
2) Reviewing the Business Planning and updating annual action and budgeting priorities for the next 12 months
3) Updating the success of the Strategic Management System itself, the Strategic Change Leadership Team and the Strategy Project Teams
4) Reviewing and problem solving the status of the vital few strategic change leverage points, to Create Customer Value (See Seven Elements/Modules of the Business Excellence Architecture for details)

The key to sustaining a customer-focused high performance organization over the long term is this formal yearly review and update. It is another step most often overlooked by executives.

The specific Annual Strategic Review and Update step includes four pieces:

1) Contracting and Plan-to-Review with an outside consultant/impartial observer
2) Conduct a strategic review and diagnosis; both statistically, interviews and observations
3) Synthesize data, write the report and make recommendations for improvement
4) Hold two Strategic Change Leadership Team meetings of two days each (estimated), to update the Business Plan

Standard Agenda for Two Business Planning Update Meetings:
• Receive the report and feedback
• Discuss its recommendations
• Conduct a Future Environmental Scan
• Start to update your Business Plan. Re-confirm and/or refine your Vision, Mission, Values, Success Measures, and Core Strategies
• Conduct a Current State Assessment (SWOT analysis)
• Make decisions regarding next steps, focusing on the "vital few leverage points for strategic change and the Customer Value "Star Results" positioning
• Set new action plans and priorities for each core strategy to guide this next year's Annual Planning and Budgeting process
• Make decisions regarding future strategic process and structural mechanisms to guide the next year change process, while building the next year Yearly Comprehensive Map of Implementation

After the Business Planning Update Meetings:

After these offsite meetings, integrate changes into the:
a. Monthly Strategic Change Leadership Team meetings,
b. Specific strategic change projects, as well as
c. Day-to-day tasks, and
d. Weekly executive team staff meetings in order to ensure sustained achievement of our Vision over time.

Annual Strategic IQ™ Audit and Certification

Every organization and Business Unit has a yearly Financial Audit and Certification. This is important, but it is a backwards look at history. A Strategic IQ™ Audit is forward looking. For details, see our free article on this topic at the Haines Centre for Strategic Management's website (www.HainesCentre.com).

CHAPTER 13
Engineering Success Up-Front

Three Ways to Get Started in Strategic Management

There are three main ways to get started with creating your customer-focused organization.

OPTION A - Plan-to-Plan: The usual first method is a one day Executive Briefing and Plan-to-Plan event (Step #1). This is an inexpensive educating, assessing, organizing and tailoring opportunity. This decision-making day pursues four objectives:

1. To gain a common set of principles and knowledge about how to Reinvent Business Planning in the 21st Century, through a morning Executive Briefing.

2. To understand how reinventing Business Planning is really a Strategic Management System, and what that means in terms of our Three Goals towards Creating a Customer-Focused High Performance Organization.

3. To diagnose your strategic issues and to examine certain components of your current Business Plans as a way to tailor your Business Planning and Strategic Management process.

4. To conduct an actual "Plan-to-Plan" work session in the afternoon, in order to determine next steps, if any, for a tailored and crafted Business Planning process that meets your unique situation and needs.

OPTION B - Plan-to-Implement: The second way to get started is the one day Plan-To-Implement day (Step #8). Afterwards, you will be more organized for implementation and change (Step #9). During the first year of implementation, the Strategic Change Leadership Team takes the lead in identifying and completing those aspects of the full Business Planning process that make sense to them. This should be done at Annual Strategic Review and Update sessions (Step #10).

OPTION C - Tailored to your needs: Begin anywhere you want on our Five Phase ABCDE Business Planning and Strategic Management process and then continue on from there, filling in the blanks as you go. For example:

Using the Systems Thinking Approach°and framework, lets you enter your system at any point that needs assistance, including:

1. Set up a Strategic Change Leadership Team to guide and coordinate existing change

2. Conduct annual planning via Core Strategies with top three yearly action priorities for each

3. Finish budgeting and then set up Strategic Change Project Teams on big, cross-functional issues

4. Have internal staff trained and licensed on Business Planning facilitation

5. Have internal staff get trained and licensed on Leading Strategic Change

6. Conduct a Visionary Leadership Practices Workshop to "kick-start" Business Planning

7. Conduct a Leading Strategic Change Workshop simulation to "kick-start" or re-energize a major change project

8. Conduct a pilot Business Planning process for a major support department or a Strategic Business Unit. Use it to learn and to develop internal cadre

9. Conduct only the Business Planning phase you need now – such as Visioning, measurements (Key Success Measures) or Core Strategy (issues) development... and then put in a Strategic Change Leadership Team to guide implementation

10. Get your management trained in Business Planning concepts through a 2-3 day workshop on Reinventing Business Planning for the 21st Century

11. Conduct your management conference keynoted with a Business Planning/Strategic Change, one-two hour topic, using our four-color models and four page summary articles as handouts

12. Have an Annual Strategic Review and Update conducted as a starting point. Then proceed based on the recommendations/decisions from this audit

In any case, remember that this is a long term process of success. Quick fixes are not lasting.

This Systems Thinking Approach° is a multi-year change effort to Create Customer Value and achieve your Ideal Future Vision on an ongoing basis.

Final Summary

As a final summary, here are 15 Absolutes for
Strategic Management Implementation Success.

The Tools, Tips, and Techniques for Successful Implementation

1. Have a clear vision and values – of your Ideal future with customer-focused outcomes/measures.

2. Develop focused core strategies – as the glue for setting and reviewing annual goal setting and action planning for all major departments/SBUs.

3. Set up "Strategic Project Teams" – of cross-functional leaders to develop, track, and monitor each core strategy.

4. Focus on and phase in the Vital Few Leverage Points – for Strategic Change over the next 2-5 years, starting with leadership skill building immediately – and then focus on being a "Star" in "value-added delivery."

5. Create a critical mass for change – that "goes ballistic" and becomes self-sustaining through development of Three-Year Business Plans for all major divisions/departments.

6. Develop and gain public commitments of "Personal Leadership Plans" by all top management leaders – then communicate, communicate, communicate.

7. Set up an "internal cadre" support team – with overall change management coordination reporting directly to the CEO/Executive Director.

8. Establish a Strategic Change Leadership Team – led by the CEO – with a yearly Process Map – that meets on a regular monthly basis to guide, lead, and manage all major changes.

9. Redo your HR Management Systems – to support the new vision/values, especially your performance/rewards system and performance appraisal form (evaluate each employee vs. core values and core strategies).

10. Institutionalize the Parallel Involvement Process – with all key stakeholders as the new participative way you plan, change, and run your business day-to-day.

11. Set up KSMs and a Tracking System – to ensure clarity/focus on the

scoreboard for success

12. Use a Consistent Annual Planning Format – to link strategies/priorities to annual plans and results

13. Set the Top Annual Priorities – on only 2 pages to focus everyone on what's important next year

14. Conduct Annual Large Group Review Meetings – each year to ensure everyone knows and is "in sync" with everyone else

15. Conduct the Annual Strategic Review and Update – like an independent financial audit to ensure constant updating of your Business Plan as a living document

Getting started on turning your unit into a "Customer-Focused High Performance Learning Organization" should use all of the points in this Business Planning Guide. However, it is still very difficult to stay focused on the "Vital Few" Leverage Points for change versus our "Trivial Many" daily tasks. To remain consistent in managing within the System's Thinking Framework articulated here requires more than good intentions. As Ed Lawlor states in his book, The Ultimate Advantage: Creating the High Involvement Organization:

Conclusion:

"Sometimes having a good management system is confused with having high-quality employees. This is a mistake - the two are quite different in some important ways: Having high-quality employees does not assure an organization of having a sustainable competitive advantage."

Thus, our final argument in this Guide is that today's executives desiring to develop high performing customer-focused organizations need to install a "Strategic Management System" as a new way to run their business day-to-day.

In the traditional roles senior management has played, perhaps only 5-10% of their time were on strategic issues. However, in today's revolutionary changing environment, senior management must spend a good portion of their time (20% or more) on strategy and strategic thinking, and then use that to STRATEGICALLY MANAGE the business unit/functional area as an entire SYSTEM (i.e. a Strategic Management System).

This is what the Haines Centre for Strategic Management does best. We help visionary senior executives and top management teams develop and institutionalize this System.

This Strategic Management System is our way to assist these executives in Creating Customer-Focused High Performance Organizations. Through our Strategic Planning, Business Planning and Change Management, we help align organizations and their people in delivering real value to their customers.

This means putting special emphasis on choosing successful strategies, and then Focusing on these Vital Few Leverage Points that translate into results. Balancing the processes required to achieve this, along with the right strategies and content-focus for the organization, is the art and "jazz" of the strategic changes desired.

Ultimately, it is Senior Management's Leadership and the organization's Human Resource programs and practices that must be in sync or in proper attunement. This attunement ensures that the customer-focused Vision makes the "organization as a system" function together effectively. Again, the key to this is Focusing on the five "Star Results" Positioning that customers desire, and working backwards through the organization to deliver these customer wants and needs, the first time and every time.

Successful navigation of the turbulent waters in today's highly competitive and global marketplace demands this type of integrated Systems Thinking Approach to creating and sustaining a Strategic Management System as your competitive advantage.

As a final thought, view this Business Planning Guide as your compass toward defining and implementing the tough choices that are required by sound strategic management. To avoid tough choices is to let the future success of your organization be determined by circumstances that are increasingly beyond your control. Our proven best practices and systems approach gives you the necessary tools to successfully lead the designing, building, and sustaining of your Ideal Future Vision as a customer-focused high performance learning organization.

Are you ready to develop the disciplined
Systems Thinking Approach®
needed to create a customer-focused,
high-performance business unit?

*"What we think,
or what we know,
or what we believe is,
in the end,
of little consequence...*

*The only consequence
is what we do!"*

"Good luck in developing your Strategic Management System, and achieving outstanding results."

CHAPTER 14
Facilitation Tips

Key Tips on "Facilitating Closure" in Executive Groups

1. Set up ground rules in the beginning; especially consensus = "actively support"
2. Have a one-to-one conversation with the CEO about the bottom line of participation and participative management
3. Get closure by being focused and disciplined. Force the discussions to one topic at a time List all topics on a flip chart
4. Get closure on easy topics first to get both positive movement and to isolate the difficult issues until last
5. Wait to talk or intervene until they start repeating their ideas – i.e., saying the same thing or "going around the barn" a second time
6. Test for closure – "I may be wrong, but are you saying that…"
7. Take a neutral position; help them get an answer that makes sense or is logical for them
8. Getting closure is the goal – be non-judgmental/neutral as to what it is
9. Stay above the debate; don't get caught up in one-to-one's with participants
10. Often it is best to just sit and observe for ten minutes or more. Let them discuss and frame the issues; you just actively listen
11. Follow where the energy takes them – passion vs. logic. Passion is great in support of the decision, but be sure logic backs it up. Be a devil's advocate; ask "dumb" questions
12. Randomly write down logic patterns on a flip chart; often the answer emerges
13. Don't skip over resistance. Go into it by asking "why" – have them explain the logic/rationale behind their opinion
14. Your job is to make it easy for the group to focus and talk openly. Protect the minority point of view
15. Impartiality is key. When you have a bias, turn it into an open-ended question instead
16. Too much content expertise can be a liability, as can too much commitment to the organization. Be calm, centered, neutral, and focus on process

17. Come back later to reaffirm and solidify/clarify the earlier decision; two consensus checks – i.e., sleep on it!
18. Root out hidden agendas: Ask "Why?" up to five times
19. Influence often goes to whoever has the last word
20. Ask them to collaborate on reaching consensus and closure; you can't do it alone. In the extreme: "If you don't focus on closure, why should I? It's your meeting"
21. Go around the room to give everyone a chance to be heard. Closure often emerges as you do this
22. Even the CEO must share the logic of his/her opinions and decisions. Is he/she willing to listen, be naive, learn, and be wrong?
23. "Premature shut down or quick closures" instead of working to closure is the novice's worst move. Only the group can make this decision. Instead of shutting down differences prematurely, ask permission for shut down (along with next steps and when to finish closure). You can also give advance signals/comments that time is about up and ask for help with the process/next steps/closure.

CHAPTER 15
Summary: Recap of Key Points and Checklists

Overall Three-Year Business Planning:
Recap of Key Points

- Looking at your organization as having at least three levels: individual, group, and organization – you'll need to "cascade" your planning and change management down to all levels.

- Business planning should lead the way in integrating many of today's organizational change fads and concepts, such as TQM, business process reengineering, empowerment, customer service.

- Which of these 15 Strategic Management mistakes have you made?

  1. Failing to integrate planning at all levels

  2. Keeping planning separate from day-to-day management

  3. Conducting long-range forecasting only

  4. Having a scattershot approach to planning

  5. Developing vision, mission, and value statements that are little more than fluff

  6. Having yearly weekend retreats as your only planning activity

  7. Failing to complete an effective implementation process

  8. Violating the "people support what they help create" principle

  9. Conducting business as usual after business planning

  10. Failing to make the "touch choices"

  11. Lacking a scoreboard. Measuring what's easy; not what's important

  12. Failing to define Strategic Business Units in a meaningful way

  13. Neglecting to benchmark yourself against the competition

  14. Seeing the planning document as an end in itself

  15. Having confusing terminology and language

- Which of these benefits are still missing in your unit?

  1. Having an unit-wide, proactive approach to a changing global world

  2. Building an executive team that serves as a model of cross-functional or horizontal teamwork

  3. Having an intense executive development and orientation process

  4. Defining focused, quantifiable outcome measures of success

  5. Making intelligent budgeting decisions

  6. Clarifying your competitive advantage

  7. Reducing conflict; empowering the organization

  8. Providing clear guidelines for day-to-day decision making

  9. Creating a critical mass for change

  10. "Singing from the same hymnal" in communicating throughout

  11. Clarifying and simplifying the broad range of management techniques

  12. Empowering middle managers

  13. Focusing everyone in the organization on the same overall priorities

  14. Speeding up implementation of your core strategies

  15. Providing tangible tools for dealing with the stress of change

Overall Three-Year Business Planning:
Recap of Key Points *(continued)*

- Evaluate your SBUs/MPAs/MFAs to determine if any are outside your driving force(s) and core strategies/competencies

- Ascertain which SBUs/MPAs/MFA will need to change or be added in order to fulfill your organizational mission statement

- Make sure you know the risk involved, and have specific plans to deal with it

- Bring every step of your SBU/MPA/MFA planning back to your organization-wide core strategies

- Limit your new business development searches to no more than 15-20% of your total effort and resources

- In your Three-Year Business Unit Planning, be sure to follow the same systems thinking, A-B-C-D-E five-phase process as in your overall strategic planning

- Incorporate new product development in your Business Unit Planning

- Identify the market segmentation of each Business Unit Planning or service, and develop support strategies that include the four "P's" of marketing

- Be sure to accommodate the support needs of each SBU Business Plan

Overall Three-Year Business Planning
Action Checklist

1. Define the SBUs/MPAs that currently exist in your organization

2. Define the present revenue/profitability expectations of each SBU/MPA

3. Delineate the desired future of each SBU/MPA, along with their future revenue/profits at the end of your planning horizon

4. Develop criteria for SBU or MPA selection/exclusion/dropping, especially the customer/market research

5. Analyze each SBU/MPA based on that criteria; incorporate some traditional analysis tools as well (i.e., risk/focus/etc.)

6. Force-rank a set of priorities of the remaining SBU/MPAs

7. Analyze these decisions from a holistic perspective; make sure you haven't lost any core competencies by selective individual decisions

8. For those SBU/MPAs dropped or excluded, make a choice to either say "no" to the customer – or develop strategic alliances/partnerships with others to provide for them

9. Establish goals/targets for overall organization growth rates of volume and profitability

10. Establish an ongoing system to manage the changes resulting from your prioritization

11. Develop product/market plans, organization structure, teams, and budgets to achieve your SBU/MPA targets; then adjust or reiterate this cycle where necessary to match resources with targets

Three Main Premises

Main Premise #1:

"Planning and Change are the Primary Job of Leaders"

Main Premise #2:

"People Support What They Help Create"

Main Premise #3:

"Use Systems Thinking" – Focus on Outcomes: The Customer

Three Primary Goals of Any Organization/Unit

GOAL #1:
Develop a Business Plan/Document

GOAL #2:
Ensure its Successful Implementation and Change

GOAL #3:
Build and Sustain High Performance
Over the Long Term, Year After Year

THE SYSTEMS THINKING APPROACH®
"The Natural Way the World Works"

"A New Orientation to Life" – Our Core Technology
STRATEGIC THINKING
"From Complexity to Simplicity"

Systems: Systems are made up of a set of components that work together for the overall objective of the whole (output).

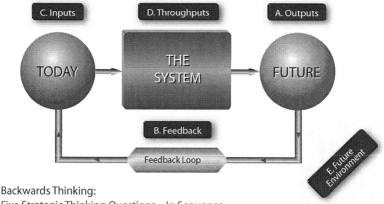

Backwards Thinking:
Five Strategic Thinking Questions – In Sequence:

A Where do we want to be? (i.e., our ends, outcomes, purposes, goals, holistic vision)

B How will we know when we get there? (i.e., the customers' needs and wants connected into a quantifiable feedback system)

C Where are we now? (i.e., today's issues and problems)

D How do we get there? (i.e., close the gap from C ➡ A in a complete, holistic way)

E Ongoing:
What will/may change in your environment in the future?

vs. Analytic Thinking Which:

1 Starts with today and the current state, issues, and problems

2 Breaks the issues and/or problems into their smallest components

3 Solves each component separately (i.e., maximizes the solution)

4 Has no far-reaching vision or goal (just the absence of a problem)

NOTE: In Systems Thinking, the whole is primary and the parts are secondary (not vice-versa).

"If you don't know where you're going, any road will get you there."

Why Thinking Matters
"How you think... is how you act... is how you are."

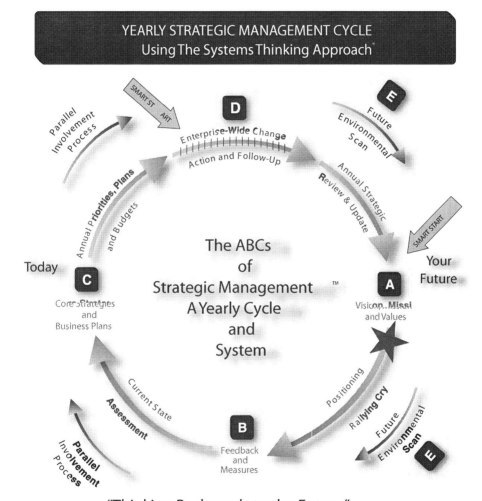

YEARLY STRATEGIC MANAGEMENT CYCLE
Using The Systems Thinking Approach

"Thinking Backwards to the Future"

Plan-to-Plan (Step #1)
Recap of Key Points

- Before you begin the Plan-to-Plan step, make sure you are clear on what it is, i.e., an "Executive Briefing" and an opportunity to organize your approach to the strategic planning process (educate and organize)

- Be specific and clear on the exact entity for which you're going to plan (organization, geographic community sector, business unit, etc.)

- Identify the key issues that are critical to your organization's success up front, as a guide to keeping planning practical. Use the strategic/organizational assessment to accomplish this

- Make sure the top members of your collective leadership are personally ready and committed to leading your strategic planning and change management process. In other words, conduct capacity-building through team-building/visionary leadership priorities and skills training, right away

- Use Plan-to-Plan as an opportunity to problem-solve potential barriers to strategic/business planning your organization may encounter, before you begin

- Be sure to scan your organization's environment, both internal and external, to make certain you're not trying to create your plan in a vacuum

- Don't blindly follow the ten steps of the planning model; tailor your strategic plan in a way that best fits your particular organization

- Make sure your strategic/business plan drives your budget, not vice versa. Be sure to sequence them over your yearly cycle

- Your key stakeholders should include anyone who affects or is affected by the organization's strategic plan

- Don't let your planning team grow beyond 12 individuals

- Create a staff support cadre to support the planning team

- Have an experienced strategic/business planning facilitator who can play devil's advocate and facilitate strong egos

- Incorporate a Parallel Involvement Process to integrate the planning team's progress with other key stakeholders, inside and out of the organization. Communicate...communicate...communicate!

- Set up clear, mutually agreed-upon ground rules that will be in effect for the entire planning and implementation process

- Review and reaffirm all commitments to your organization's plan and the planning process, including the three goals

- Take 3-5 minutes and the end of each planning day to give yourselves feedback, and to learn from your experiences.
  Ask the 3 key questions:

  1. What can we continue to do?

  2. What can we do more of?

  3. What should we do less of?

Plan-to-Plan Tasks (Step #1)
Action Checklist

- "Look before you leap." Have at least a half-day "Executive Briefing," in which all top management executives, including the CEO, understand and are in sync with the planning process. Consider including key stakeholders in this, as well

- Hold a 'kick off' meeting to share with all key stakeholders the planning process and their role in it

- Select an external strategic/business planning facilitator to start the planning process, but also set up the staff support cadre right away, so you can eventually have the internal capacity to run this process yourself

- Complete all the Plan-to-Plan tasks either in a formal, half-day session following the Executive Briefing session, or informally with the CEO and top management team

Use this list of 25 tasks as your checklist:

1. Organization specifications sheet

2. A high performance organization mini survey

3. Pre-work strategic planning briefing questionnaire

4. Executive briefing on Strategic Management

5. Personal readiness for Strategic Management

6. Strategic planning problems/barriers

7. Readiness actions and steps

8. Organizational fact sheet for strategic planning

9. Strategic issues list

10. Strategic planning staff support team/needed meetings

11. Planning team membership

12. Identification of key stakeholders

13. Key stakeholder involvement

14. Initial environmental scanning/current state assessment required (7 minimum areas)

15. Reinvented Strategic Planning Model tailored to your needs

16. Strategic planning link to budgets

17. Organizational and individual leadership (self-change)

18. Individual commitment

19. Strategic implementation and change commitments

20. Strategic planning updates communicated to others

21. Energizers for meetings

22. Strategic planning meeting process observer

23. Action minutes format

24. Meeting processing guide

25. Closure/action planning

Future Environmental Scanning: Phase E :

This Phase E is often missed. Use the SKEPTIC Framework, set up teams for each letter, and conduct a Future Scan, sharing all of the information for trends that are gathered.

Reinvented Strategic Management (Step #1)
(Tailored To Your Needs)

Based on your current understanding of the Busines Planning and Change Management Models (and Strategic Management), please list the importance (H-M-L) of developing each potential deliverable for your Business Unit, Major Program Area, or Major Functional Area.

Business Planning – Steps #2-5 (Phases E-A-B-C)

1. _____   Environmental Scanning

2. _____   Vision – Our Ideal Future, Aspirations, Guiding Star

3. _____   Mission – Who, What, Why We Exist

4. _____   Values – Our Guiding Principles, To Guide Organizational Behaviors

5. _____   Driving Force(s) – Positioning, Our Competitive Edge

5a._____   Rallying Cry – 3-6 Key Motivational Words

6. _____   Key Success Measures – Quantifiable Measures of Success

7. _____   Current State Assessment

8. _____   Core Strategies – Major Means, Approaches, Methods to Achieve Our Vision

9. _____   Actions/Yearly Priorities Under Each Core Strategy

Annual Plans – Step #7 (Phase C)

10. _____   Annual Plans/Priorities/Department Plans

11. _____   Resource Allocation/Strategic Budgeting - including guidelines

Individuals/Teams

12. _____   Individual Performance Management System – Tied to Business Planning

12a._____   Rewards and Recognition System – Tied to Business Planning

Bridge the Gap – Step #8 (Phase D)

13. _____   Plan-to-Implement Day – Get Educated, Assess, Organize and Tailor Our Change Management Process/Structures, Tailored Game Plan

Focus on the Vital Few (Phase D) – Star Positioning Model

14a. _____ Quality Products and Services

14b. _____ Customer Service

14c. _____ Speed/Responsiveness/Convenience for the Customer

14d. _____ Choice, Fashion, Control, Customized

14e. _____ Low Price and Costs

Alignment of Delivery – Step #9 (Phase D)

15a. _____ Organization Structure/Redesign

15b. _____ Business Process Reengineering – customer focused to lower costs and improve response

15c. _____ Blow Out Bureaucracy and Waste - Simply - Simplify

15d. _____ Information Technology – Technology Steering Group

Attunement of People/Support Systems – Step #9 (Phase D)

16a. _____ Professional Management and Leadership Competencies, Skills

16b. _____ Management Change Skills/Managing Strategic Change Skills

16c. _____ HR Programs/Processes – Employee Development Board

16d. _____ Values/Cultural Change Skills

16e. _____ Employee Involvement/Participative Management Skills/Empowerment

16f. _____ Strategic Communications: Knowledge and Skills

Annual Strategic Review & Yearly Update – Step #10 (Phase D)

17. _____ Annual Strategic Review and Update

Teamwork (Throughout)

18a. _____ Teamwork for Executive Team

18b. _____ Teamwork for Department Teams

18c. _____ Teamwork for Cross-Functional Relationships/Teams

18d. _____ Strategic Alliances

Phase A - Ideal Future Vision (Step #2)
Recap of Key Points

- The Ideal Future Vision step is the first real action step in strategic planning, and one of the recurring key elements for success

- The first challenge in the Ideal Future Vision step is to shape an organizational "vision statement"

- The second challenge is a realistic "mission statement" that describes your organization's desired, unique purpose

- The third challenge is the development of "core values" that make up your organization's culture: "What we believe in"

- Challenge #4 is designing a "rallying cry," or driving force, which states the essence of your organization: its raison d'être. It is often better to wait until the end of strategic planning, in order to really clarify the essence of your strategic plan

- It will be necessary to identify and assess the levels of risk inherent in these challenges

- Avoid these five major areas of confusion in developing a mission:

  1. Mistaking the "how" as being part of the mission
  2. Failing to focus on the customer
  3. Lack of clarity on "control" vs. "service" in departmental mission statements
  4. Failing to properly define your "entity" in the public sector.
  5. "Going through the motions" only

- In developing your vision and mission statements, it is critical that you clearly define your customer in specific terms

- Every component in the Ideal Future Vision step is important, as part of an overall, cohesive whole

- The Ideal Future Vision is necessary but not sufficient for success. You must go further with the full strategic plan, annual plan, implementation and change

Ideal Future Vision (Step #2)
Action Checklist

- Develop a vision statement that "gets outside the nine dots" and expresses your ideal future as an organization/business unit

- Create a mission statement that clearly identifies the who, what, and why of your organization

- Make sure your vision and mission statements relate closely to the day-to-day realities of your organization

- As you shape your vision and mission statements, be certain you keep your customer clearly defined and in focus

- Develop a set of core organizational values that you can adhere to, organization-wide, through the long-term

- Define your current organizational culture, and the number of subculture levels throughout the organization

- Create an action plan that will enable you to shape a culture that is consistent throughout the organization

- Define your organization's driving force, so that you can develop an organization-wide, motivational rallying cry

- Make sure your organization's rallying cry contains the essence of your vision, mission, and values statements

- Assess the level of risk involved in making these changes and take an honest inventory of your willingness to change

Phase B : Key Success Measures/Goals (Step #3)
Recap of Key Points

- Be sure to reflect the customer's point of view, both internally and externally

- Measure all key elements of your Ideal Future Vision

- Focus on outputs and results, except possibly, for some crucial benchmarking on processes/systems

- Benchmarking vs. the competition may or may not be organization wide KSMs. However, at the business unit level of the organization, they definitely are Key Success Measures, and should be tracked and evaluated as such

- Be careful on competitive benchmarks, as rarely do two firms in the same business sector function in exactly the same fashion

- Be sure to use the Parallel Involvement Process for KSMs as well; ownership and buy-in are essential

- Cost/benefits analysis applies to KSM development also. Use readily available data when at all possible

- If your vision and mission should change at any point, remember to change your KSMs accordingly

- KSMs are often something new; it may take a year or so to get used to working with them and to get just the right measurement. Consider them cast in sand at first; concrete later. So, don't publicly broadcast the exact targets too soon

- Some KSMs, like performance improvements, are a long-term process; just tracking and measuring in the first year is a good result. Have patience

- Tie your executive bonus or incentive pay and rewards to KSMs. This could be a separate project, but it is vitally important to success

- All performance appraisal forms should be tied to your core values (behaviors), as well as to the KSMs/strategies (results)

- Since KSMs are outcomes/results, they are often seen as goals or objectives, and the words can sometimes be used interchangeably. Be clear on your terms

Key Success Measures/Goals (Step #3)
Action Checklist

- Determine your KSM/Goal areas, based on vision, values, mission, and driving force(s). Do it first individually, then in subgroups, then the total group

- Set specific KSM factors and measures (targets) for end-of-planning-horizon (i.e., the year 2009), baseline year (current year), and even intermediate targets if possible. If you don't have enough time, do these later...but do them...set a deadline

- Assign KSM accountability for each KSM and also an overall KSM Coordinator for total accountability to collect and report the data

- Troubleshoot your KSMs to ensure they are outputs/results/core values, vs. means-to-an-end. Means should only be used when ends can't be measured effectively or the means are absolutely essential

- Define/agree on priorities for the KSMs, i.e., forced ranking of 10 or less

- Eliminate the lowest priority KSMs if they are not critical or you have too many (10 is maximum)

- If you do not currently have the measure in place, your target for the first year will be to set it up and establish it on an ongoing basis

- Wherever possible, be sure to benchmark your KSMs against your competitors' best practices

- Set up the reporting format for KSMs and use it to track ongoing progress of target vs. actual

- Establish a measurement to find out whether the plan and the total strategic management system has become a practical reality, just like a yearly independent financial audit

Phase C : Current State Assessment (Step #4)
Recap of Key Points

- When conducting your internal and external assessments, be willing to honestly accept all findings, not just the positive ones

- In your internal Current State Assessment, be sure to include thorough evaluation of these ten points:

  1. Organization financial analysis
  2. Core values analysis
  3. Key Success Measure analysis
  4. Organization design
  5. Business process reengineering
  6. Management/leadership
  7. Key Human resource areas
  8. Reward for total performance
  9. Teamwork
  10. Core competencies

- In your external Current State Assessment, be sure to include an evaluation of these ten areas:

  1. Stakeholder analysis
  2. Organizational life cycle
  3. Industry structure analysis
  4. Competitor analysis
  5. Strategic Business Unit (SBU) information
  6. Customer focus
  7. Market orientation and segmentation
  8. Value map of products and services (positioning)
  9. Market share and growth rate
  10. Product/market certainty

- Be sure to conduct a SWOT analysis (with action implications) as a summary, to digest

Current State Assessment (Step #4)
Action Checklist

- Analyze your business unit finances and core values. Evaluate them on their capacity to support your Ideal Future Vision
- Study your organization's/business unit's design to determine if it will "get you where you want to go"
- Evaluate your unit processes from your customer's point of view
- Make sure you have the management and leadership skills you'll need
- Look at organizational reward systems, both financial and non-financial
- In conducting your Current State Assessment, it is best to utilize cross-functional teams, or other key stakeholders, to get a full picture of your organization's current performance. Prior to starting the assessment, decide which Current State Assessment tasks you want to conduct, then set up cross-functional teams to do the actual work
- Scrutinize organizational/business unit's core competencies
- Identify your external key stakeholders, and decide your responses to them in order to stay focused on your Ideal Future Vision
- Analyze what phases your unit and industry life cycles are in currently
- Make an in-depth analysis of your competition
- Defend why each of your Strategic Business Unit's should continue to exist
- In your market orientation analysis, make sure you are concentrating on your most profitable customer base. Also, determine whether your unit is structured around customer-focused units
- Develop a Value Map of your products or services, and define their market position
- Do an in-depth analysis of your current market share, and define how much your future market share should be
- Look closely at each product line; determine the implications or risks inherent in any changes you may make
- Complete your internal and external Current State Assessments with a Strengths, Weaknesses, Opportunities, Threats (SWOT) Analysis

Phase C D : Core Strategy Development (Step #5)
Recap of Key Points

- Your organization will need to develop a small number (3-7) of core strategies for bridging the gaps between your Ideal Future Vision and your Current State Assessment.
- When developing your strategies, consider these newer strategies for the 21st century:
  1. Flexibility
  2. Speed
  3. Horizontally-integrated products
  4. Networks and alliances
  6. Environmentally-improved products
  7. Mass customization
  8. Commonization/simplification
  9. Organizational learning
  10. Employee morale/benefits
  11. Roll-ups
  12. Experiences
  13. Value Chain Management
- There are five generic core strategy areas you need to consider:
  1. Product-driven strategies
  2. Market-driven strategies
  3. Financial-driven strategies
  4. Uniquely-driven strategies
  5. Employee-driven strategies
- In order to successfully reinvent your strategic planning and implementation process, you must make accommodation for the Rollercoaster of Change™.
- Integrate "building" and "cutting" (i.e., financial only) strategies...remember, you've got to "play to win!"

Annual Organization-Wide Priorities (Step #6)

- Have corresponding Action Items prioritized over the next 12 months for each of your Core Strategies.
- Create Strategy Sponsorship Teams that will "champion" each core strategy.

Core Strategy Development (Step #5)
Action Checklist

- Ascertain that your vision, mission, core values, and Current State Assessment (including SWOT) are final, then develop your new core strategies

- Develop a small number (3-7) of core strategies for implementing your organization's strategic plan. Make sure they serve you as follows:

  1. They should define your competitive business advantages, leading to long-term, sustainable organizational viability

  2. They should help you determine your overall unit design and structure, along with individual job design, employee initiative characteristics, and philosophy

  3. They should act as the "glue," or yearly objectives, around which you'll organize your annual planning process

- Develop core strategies that accommodate change, including both cutting and building strategies

- Ensure your organization has clarity of any "from-to" paradigm shifts that will result from your new core strategies

- Finalize your firm's driving force and Key Success Measures

- Develop cross-functional teams of change agents, called Strategy Project Teams, led by senior management. Assign a volunteer senior member of the core planning team as a "champion" for each core strategy

Annual Organization-Wide Priorities (Step #6)

- Each strategy should have its own Action Items carried out over the life of the planning horizon. Once they are agreed upon, set the 3-5 top action priorities for each strategy over the next 12 months. If you have six core strategies, you should have only three top priorities each

- As soon as you've finished your list of top priority actions, make a list from this list of actions to be taken in the next week, month, or quarter; do NOT sacrifice the implementation of your new strategic plan to hesitation, confusion, or inaction!

- Remember to take each stage of your strategy development through a Parallel Involvement Process, giving all levels of your organization's workforce the opportunity to buy into their plan

Phase $\boxed{C}$: Annual Plans and Strategic Budgets (Step #7) Recap of Key Points

- To develop an effective annual plan, you need to make sure everyone focuses on organization-wide core strategies, not on separate department or turf issues

- Make sure your actions for each core strategy support the top priority Strategic Action Items identified by senior management

- In the Large Group Review, your collective leadership should compare all annual plans against your vision, mission, values, strategies, and Key Success Measures

- In strategic budgeting, allocation of funds is determined by priorities that are crucial to the achievement of your organizational vision, rather than by department or division power struggles

- Study the different, proactive approaches to reallocating your organization's funds in a more focused way

- To cut costs in order to eliminate waste, you need to first define it. Waste is anything other than the minimum amount of equipment, people, materials, parts, space, overhead, and work time essential for added-value in your products or services

- When seeking structural changes to do business at a lower costs, don't only look in the "now" – project into the future and consider possibilities from all angles

- More and more, organizations in the public sector are finding ways to be more proactive and raise money themselves, rather than waiting for funding

- To ensure employee motivation and commitment to your plan, be sure you have both a performance management system and a rewards and recognition system in place

- In moving from planning to implementation, create a sense of ownership among employees through a rallying cry contest

Annual Plans and Strategic Budget (Step #7)
Action Checklist

• Prioritize Action Items under each strategy; use your core strategies as the organizing principles of your annual plans

• Develop departmental annual plans, including all senior department heads

• Have your collective leadership (your top 30-50 people) actively participate in a large group annual plan review and problem-solving meeting

• Your top executives (i.e., CEO, President, COO, Superintendent, Executive Director, etc.) should present their Personal Leadership Plans of what tasks they will personally do to help guide the plan's implementation

• At the close of your Large Group Review, be sure that each participant prepares and presents one or two quick, easy actions they will take under each strategy over the next two weeks

• Review and adopt some of the ten ways to establish your approach to budgeting and resource allocation

• Design a performance management system that enables individuals to set goals based on the strategic plan, as well as to take accountability and responsibility for their part in the overall plan

• Create a rewards and recognition systems that reinforces employee commitment and rewards contribution, while encouraging individual success with specific, tangible rewards and/or recognition

• Bridge the gap from planning to implementation by holding an organization-wide "rallying cry" contest

Phase D : Plan-to-Implement (Step #8)
Recap of Key Points

- At the completion of your business planning, have a "Plan-to-Implement" Day with two segments: Executive Briefing and Educating, and Organizing Change Tasks

- Know the difference between simply surviving change and mastering it; developing viable change mechanisms you control over the long term

- The first cardinal rule of change is that organizations don't change, people do

- The second cardinal rule of change is that you must design and develop structures for managing change that are separate from existing, day-to-day organizational structures

- If your top management doesn't set aside the time to manage and lead your change effort, it won't go far. Employees watch what you do, and what you don't do, for clues to your real priorities

- You must prepare for and be ready to manage the four phases in the Rollercoaster of Change on a constant basis, as people change at different rates and speeds: (1) shock & denial, (2) depression, (3) hope, and (4) rebuilding

- In order for your change effort to succeed, understand that your organization is a living, breathing system and use the "Organization as a System" model to ensure system's fit, alignment, and integrity

- When initiating the implementation of your strategic/business plan, be sure to incorporate all ten key change management tasks:

    1. Strategic plan rollout
    2. Strategic Change Leadership Team
    3. Internal support cadre
    4. Allocate resources for change
    5. Yearly comprehensive map of implementation
    6. Strategy Sponsorship Teams
    7. Key Success Measure tracking
    8. Personal Leadership Plans
    9. Performance and rewards system
    10. Build a critical mass for change

- It is a critical senior management task to check your change management system for its fit, alignment, and integrity with your vision on a constant basis

- Conduct yearly updating of your strategic plan

- Conduct a yearly follow-up and diagnose overall implementation performance

Phase ☐D: Plan-to-Implement (Step #8)
Action Checklist

- Develop an initial rollout and communications plan

- Establish an organization-wide annual plan reflecting the strategic planning priorities for the first year

- Align the budget to reflect the business planning priorities

- Build all department/division/unit annual plans around the organization-wide annual priorities or goals

- Set up an ongoing Strategic Change Leadership Team to manage the change process monthly

- Establish a yearly map, or master work plan, for 12-month implementation and follow-up. It should include Three-Year Business Plans for any SBU's or major support departments that do not have such plans

- Establish a Key Success Measure monitoring, tracking, and reporting system

- Revise your performance and reward system to support your new Vision, core strategies, and values

- Put an environmental scanning system (Phase E) in place, both yearly and in quarterly Strategic Change Leadership Team meetings

- Make sure top management has an ongoing, active leadership in your change process

- Build an internal support cadre with the expertise and skills to coordinate the strategic plan's implementation and change management

- Ensure key Strategy Project Teams are set up to build a critical mass for change

Plan-to-Implement (Step #8)
Year #1: Strategic Change Process
* = Absolutes to Prevent Failure and Achieve Success

Score this H-M-L, depending on your needs.

H-M-L

_____ 1.*   Finalize the Business Plan

_____ 2.   Develop an initial rollout and communications plan

_____ 3.*   Establish an organization-wide annual plan reflecting the strategic planning "action priorities" for the first year for each Core Strategy

_____ 4.   Align the budget to reflect the strategic planning annual priorities (at least 33% effective in the first year)

_____ 5.   Build all department, division, unit annual plans around the organization-wide annual priorities and goals

_____ 6.*   Hold a peer review meeting and critique, then finalize the strategic planning

_____ 7.   Implement Three-Year Business Plans for each strategic business unit/major support division to verify, extend, and integrate the organization-wide plan

_____ 8.*   Set up an ongoing monthly "Strategic Change Leadership Team meeting" to manage the change process

_____ 9.   Set up the rest of the change management structures

_____ 10.*   Establish a "Master Work Plan" for Year #1 implementation and follow-up ("Yearly Map")

_____ 11.*   Establish a Key Success Measure coordinator for monitoring, tracking, and reporting

_____ 12.*   Revise the performance management and rewards systems as an evaluation framework to support the desired Vision

_____ 13.   Examine your organizational structure, including Employee Development Board to support the desired Vision

_____ 14.   Implement the desired change(s) in both the Headquarter's departments and in units, sites, and field locations

_____ 15.   Put an Environmental Scanning System in place

_____ 16.*   Obtain senior management's personal commitment to a set of tasks to implement the Strategic Plan (i.e., Personal Leadership Plans)

_____ 17.* Identify Internal Staff Support Team and manage their development to ensure you build your own internal cadre of expertise and the skills (not just knowledge) to carry out your vision and core values

_____ 18. Ensure key cross-department "Strategic Change Projects" are set up with clear accountability

_____ 19. Establish game plan to ensure that a critical mass in favor of the changes is established (rational, political, cultural dimensions)

_____ 20. Set in place Strategic Project Teams for each Core Strategy

_____ 21. Allocate resources to fund the change process and internal support cadre

_____ 22.* Put in place two absolutely key training and development programs with a top-down ("walk-the-talk") fashion:

_____   (a) Leading Strategic Change, and

_____   (b) Visionary Leadership Practices and Skills (and a Leadership Development System)

_____ 23.* Set up the dates and process for the Annual Strategic Review and Update including the diagnostic assessments and large group annual plans/review meeting

_____ 24. Put in place a method to reduce costs, bureaucracy, waste & other obsolete tasks, including business process reengineering.

_____ 25. Set up a specific game plan to become "customer-driven," including surveys to create customer value

_____ 26. Identify list of why our change efforts might fail
– and determine what to do to prevent this from happening

_____ 27. Establish core values assessment and action plan

_____ 28. Conduct (1) an Organization Assessment, (2) an Organization Design Study, and (3) Recommendations using "The Organization As a System" Model

_____ 29. Complete a Strategic Change Impact Exercise for each core strategy

_____ 30. Determine each department head's yearly operational "management system" to cascade this process further down into the entire organization

Phase $\boxed{D}$: Strategy Implementation and Change (Step #9)
Recap of Key Points

- In The Systems Thinking Approach®, all Strategic Management is conducted within these five A, B, C, D, E phases of the systems model:

  Phase A – Future outcomes – Where do we want to be?

  Phase B – Feedback – How will we know when we get there?

  Phase C – Today's input – Where are we now and what strategies should guide us

  Phase D – Throughput actions – How do we get there?

  Phase E – What is/might change in the Environment?

- In systems thinking, you always, always focus on the outcomes – especially the number one outcome of serving your customers

- Public sector organizations experience many of the same problems that face the private sector, and are beginning to use a business orientation and a systems approach to their planning

- In applying a business thinking approach, public sector firms face specific, contradictory issues in the following areas:

  – Mandate vs. Mission

  – Lack of a Profit Motive

  – Politicians as Board of Directors

  – Lack of a Customer Focus

  – Missing Measurements of Outcome Success

  – Parallel Involvement Process equals Public Consultation

  – Low Risk Leadership Styles

  – Perceived Resource Constraints

  – Lack of Staff Support for Strategic Management

  – Ineffective Change Management

Change Management Fail-Safe Mechanisms
44 Checks and Balances

Instructions: Review this list and make sure you have implemented all those needed. Note: an asterisk (*) denotes the "must do's" essential to success. The more of these you do, the higher your probability of successful implementation.

Do we have these?
Yes, No, or NI (needs improvement)

____ 1.* Plan-to-Plan/Executive Briefing, and "Engineer Success"
  – three goals of a Strategic Management System
____ 2.* Parallel Involvement Process throughout the planning and implementation process (key stakeholder involvement)
  – buy in; stay in
  – build critical mass for change, especially middle management
____ 3.* Three-Part Strategic Management System and Systems Thinking – a new way to run your business; the basics; an ongoing process
____ 4.* Vision, mission, core values statements in usable formats; "customer-focused"
____ 5. Cultural/values audit and the creation of a culture change action plan – strategic change project
____ 6.* Core values placed on your performance appraisal form
____ 7.* Board of Directors involvement/ownership of the strategic plan; desire to use KSMs for accountability; executive cooperation and regular status/communications to the Board
____ 8. A crisp and clear single driving force and associated rallying cry that is the essence of your vision; it is the CEO's personal task to institutionalize this
____ 9.* Key Success Measure coordinator/cadre and reporting system
____ 10.* Key Success Measure Continuous Improvement Matrix fully filled out with targets and measurements
____ 11. Benchmarking vs. highly successful organizations

_____ 12. Establishment of an Environmental Scanning System (ESS) with specific accountability and feedback mechanisms

_____ 13. SWOT with staff involvement; reality check

_____ 14.* Paradigm changes to strategies (From To) and a focused number of strategies

_____ 15.* Strategic Project Teams set up for each core strategy

_____ 16.* Core strategies also used as the Key Result Areas on performance appraisals.

_____ 17.* Annual planning format using strategies as organizing frame work (the "Glue")
  – links to strategies
  – links to values, MBO and individual goal setting/ performance appraisals

_____ 18. Use of SBU Proforma Matrix to develop clear financial accountability

_____ 19.* Three-Year Business Planning for all SBUs/MPAs/MFAs to ensure clear competitive strategies

_____ 20. SBU definition to lead organization design philosophy and efforts, focused on the businesses we are in, the customers we serve, and the employees we empower to do their best

_____ 21. Development of a Priority Maintenance System to handle interruptions, new ideas, and lack of focus on strategies, business, and product development

_____ 22.* Large group annual planning review meeting (critique/sharing)

_____ 23. Strategic Change Project Teams on big, cross-functional ideas

_____ 24.* Personal Leadership plans and commitments developed by the CEO and top three executives of the organization;

_____ 25. War Room with all the changes and time-tables on the wall

_____ 26. Contingency planning; what if scenarios on key probable events

_____ 27.* Annual planning and priority setting first to drive the budgeting process; looking at alternative ways to gain funds

_____ 28.* One day offsite: Plan-to-Implement/Executive Briefing on
Change Process

_____ 29.* Leading Strategic Change Workshop; Simulation taught
to all management personnel; indepth understanding of
change management

_____ 30.* Install different structures for change management,
including Strategic Change Leadership Team to guide:
    – Strategic Planning implementation
    – all change of any nature
The goal is System's Alignment, Attunement and Integrity

_____ 31.* Yearly Comprehensive Map on the next 12 months'
processes and structures required for change management

_____ 32.* Internal coordinator/facilitator and cadre for the change
process in support of senior management

_____ 33. Create a Critical Mass Action Plan using the Rollercoaster of
Change to support the vision, with ongoing communications
planned throughout

_____ 34.* A rollout/communications strategy plan and reinforcement
materials, led by PR or HR

_____ 35. Organization as a System framework; diagnosis and a way to
ensure System's Alignment and Integrity to the Strategic Plan
using the Business Excellence Architecture

_____ 36.* Individual goal setting by all exempt employees tied to the
Business Plan, i.e., Performance Management System
used and modeled by top management as a way to manage
individual performance as part of HR Strategic Planning

_____ 37.* A rewards diagnosis and improvement plan to ensure your
rewards support the strategic direction, both financial
and non-financial

_____ 38.*　Set up an Executive Development Committee or Board to manage promotions, executive hiring and succession plans, as well as development and training that supports the Vision, Strategic Plan, and core values/culture

_____ 39.*　Creating customer value through Business Process Reengineering action plan – Strategic Change Project

_____ 40.*　Professional management and Leadership Practices, a Strategic Leadership Development System action plan

_____ 41.　Monthly follow-up meetings to the Change Leadership Team by all departments for all employees; focus on vision, key strategies and rewards/celebrations

_____ 42.*　Organization and job redesign and restructuring action plan to be more customer-focused

_____ 43.*　Creating customer value through total quality/service action plan

_____ 44.*　Annual Strategic Review and Update, like an independent financial audit and update, of the Strategic Plan/next year's Annual Plan and priorities

Phase ⬛D⬛ : Ensuring Successful Implementation (Step #9)

Ten Key Meetings, Events, Training Programs, and Structures

1. "Visionary Leadership Practices" Training – Senior Management and Middle/First Line Managers
2. "Leading Strategic Change" Training – Senior Management and Middle/First Line Managers
3. Strategic Change Leadership Team – Meeting monthly
4. Weekly Executive Committee Meeting and Quarterly Employee Development Committee Meetings
5. Strategy Project Teams and Parallel Involvement Process Meetings with Key Stakeholders
6. Internal Cadre Support Meetings
7. Teamwork and "Cross-Functional Team Building" Training and Development – All Levels
8. Plan-to-Implement Meeting
9. Operational Planning, Large Group Annual Review Meetings, and a Strategic Budgeting Process
10. Annual Strategic Review and Update

Ten Big Change Project Tasks - Always Needed

1. Communications/rollout of the strategic plan
2. Key Success Measure development, tracking and reporting
3. Performance Management Improvement
4. Rewards and appraisals revamped
5. Total Service Management/customer-focused organization-wide
6. TQM for all products/organizational-wide as well
7. Annual Strategic Assessment
8. Organization redesign and restructuring
9. Blow out bureaucracy and waste: Simply - Simplify - Simplify
10. Build a total succession, career, and management development system

Phase $\boxed{\text{D}}$: Annual Strategic Review (Step #10)
Recap of Key Points

- Goal #3: Build and Sustain High Performance is conditional on this key step

- A key component is a new set of Annual Organization-Wide Priorities for the next 12 months under the Core Strategies to guide all Department Plans

- Financial Audits and Certification are required of all organizations. So, too, should be the Strategic IQ™ Audit and Certification

- This step should be relatively easy if the Change Leadership Team (CLT) has been meeting monthly and doing its job

- Keeping Consistency and Clarity of Purpose (Vision-Value-Positioning) is key. Varying the Core Strategies and Annual Organization-Wide Priorities is being flexible – strategic consistency and operational flexibility

– Appendix –

For the reader's benefit, we have included some additional pages of resource materials from the Centre's extensive library of visual models and reference documents. The models shown on the following pages are available in full-color, printed on 8 1/2 x 11 cards, from the Centre's publishing company, Systems Thinking Press (www.SystemsThinkingPress.com).

Ten Steps: A-B-C-D-E Applications

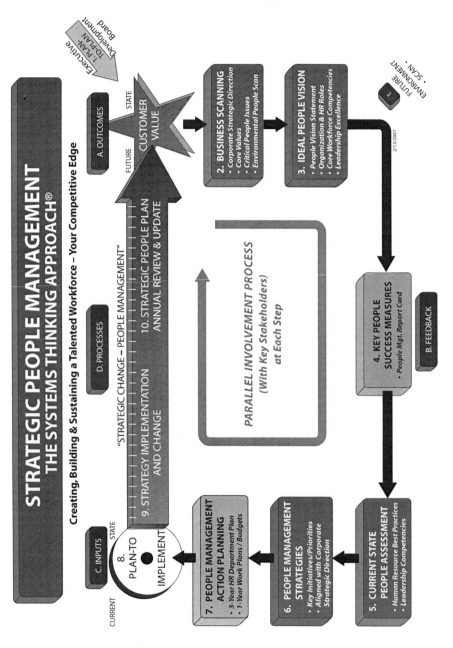

Ten Steps: A-B-C-D-E

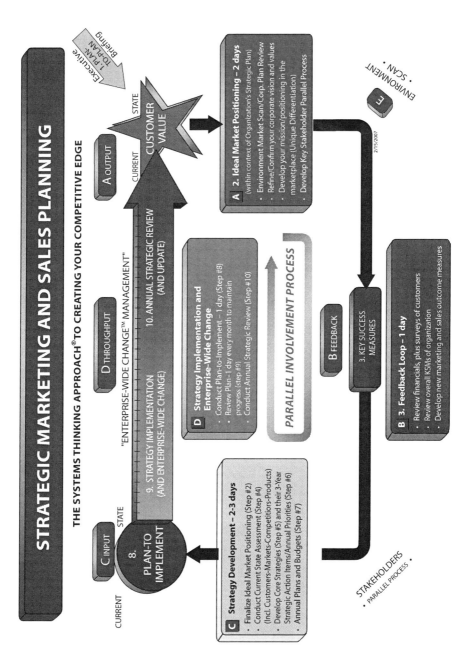

Acheiving Leadership Excellence

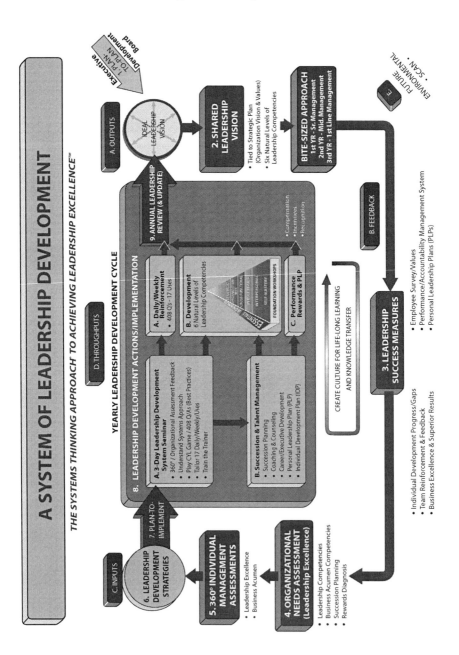

Micro Strategic Planning

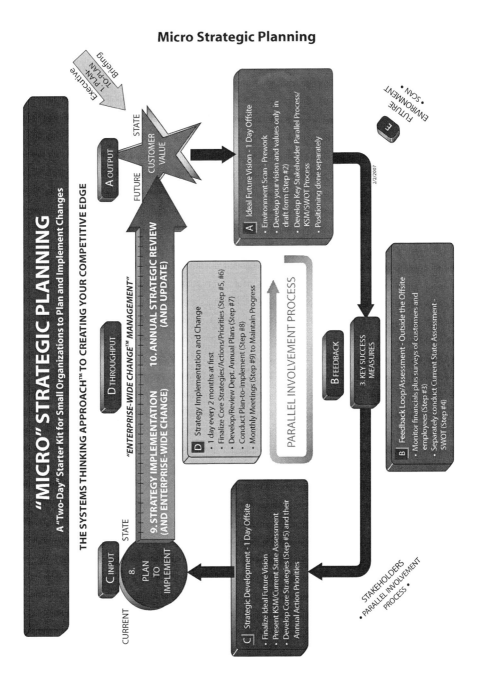

"MICRO" STRATEGIC PLANNING

A "Two-Day" Starter Kit for Small Organizations to Plan and Implement Changes

THE SYSTEMS THINKING APPROACH™ TO CREATING YOUR COMPETITIVE EDGE

"ENTERPRISE-WIDE CHANGE™ MANAGEMENT"

1. PLAN-TO-PLAN Executive Briefing

A OUTPUT — FUTURE STATE — CUSTOMER VALUE

D THROUGHPUT

C INPUT — CURRENT STATE

FUTURE ENVIRONMENT SCAN
- FUTURE ENVIRONMENT
- SCAN

A | Ideal Future Vision - 1 Day Offsite
- Environment Scan - Prework
- Develop your vision and values only in draft form (Step #2)
- Develop Key Stakeholder Parallel Process/KSM/SWOT Process
- Positioning done separately

2/2/2007

B FEEDBACK

3. KEY SUCCESS MEASURES

B | Feedback Loop/Assessment - Outside the Offsite
- Monitor financials plus surveys of customers and employees (Step #3)
- Separately conduct Current State Assessment - SWOT (Step #4)

PARALLEL INVOLVEMENT PROCESS

D | Strategy Implementation and Change
- 1 day every 2 months at first
- Finalize Core Strategies/Actions/Priorities (Step #5, #6)
- Develop/Review Dept. Annual Plans (Step #7)
- Conduct Plan-to-Implement (Step #8)
- Monthly Meetings (Step #9) to Maintain Progress

9. STRATEGY IMPLEMENTATION (AND ENTERPRISE-WIDE CHANGE)

10. ANNUAL STRATEGIC REVIEW (AND UPDATE)

8. PLAN TO IMPLEMENT

C | Strategic Development - 1 Day Offsite
- Finalize Ideal Future Vision
- Present KSM/Current State Assessment
- Develop Core Strategies (Step #5) and their Annual Action Priorities

STAKEHOLDERS PARALLEL INVOLVEMENT PROCESS

Systems Thinking Press™

Specialists in Systems Resources
www.SystemsThinkingPress.com

Ordering Information

Send Order Form to: Systems Thinking Press ~ 1420 Monitor Road ~ San Diego, CA 92110-1545

Phone: 619-275-6528 ~ **Fax:** 619-275-0324 ~ **Email:** info@SystemsThinkingPress.com ~ **Website:** www.SystemsThinkingPress.com

Date _____   If rush order, need products by _____

Name _____   Title _____

Company _____

Shipping Address _____

City _____ State _____ Postal Code _____ Country _____

Phone _____ Fax _____ Email _____

Quantity	Code	Description	Regular Price	Amount
	DT	Destination Thinking: A Business Planning Guide (Reorder)		

Sub Total	
Sales Tax (CA residents only)	
Shipping/handling charges	
TOTAL (payable in US $)	

Payment Method ~ Please Check One

Credit Cards (processed in US Dollars)   ❑ Visa   ❑ Master Card   ❑ America Express   ❑ Discover

Credit Card # _____   Expiration Date _____

Name on Card _____   Signature _____

❑ Check or Money Order Enclosed   ❑ Purchase Order (only for over $100)   PO# _____

Shipping: Please choose a shipping method below. We make every attempt to ship the cheapest and best method. If you wish to be contacted with the shipping cost prior to your order being shipped, please check here ❑

United States
- ❑ UPS Ground – 1 ½ weeks/less
- ❑ UPS Three Day (business days)
- ❑ UPS Two Day (business days)
- ❑ UPS Next Day (business days)
- ❑ US Postal Service

International
Federal Express
UPS
US Mail

- ❑ International – One week or less
- ❑ International – One week or less
- ❑ Global Priority* - 1 ½ weeks or less

- ❑ Priority International* – 2-3 days
- ❑ International Expedited* - 2-3 days
- ❑ Global Express* - One week or less

Not available in all areas.

Return Policy

You may return the products within 30 days of receipt for a refund (eProducts are not refundable). Shipping charges will not be refunded. A 20% (or greater) fee may be applied for items returned damaged. To assure proper credit, you must do three things: 1) return materials by a traceable means, 2) include a copy of your invoice, and 3) provide a reason for the return.

Our "Nothing-To-Loose Guarantee"

Our unconditional guarantee of high quality materials: if for any reason you are not satisfied with any of Haines Centre Assessments' materials, you may return them within 30 days for a refund – no questions asked.

We reserve the right to change prices without prior notice.

Systems Thinking Press
1420 Monitor Road · San Diego · CA · 92110-1545 · (619) 275-6528 · Fax (619) 275-0324
www.SystemsThinkingPress.com · Email info@SystemsThinkingPress.com